The Children's Crusade

The Children's Crusade

A History by

George Zabriskie Gray

Foreword by Thomas Powers

WILLIAM MORROW & COMPANY, INC.
New York   1972

Foreword copyright © 1972 by William Morrow and Company, Inc.

The publisher wishes to thank Virginia Coigney, Karen Hitzig, and Rodgers DePue for their help.

Printed in the United States of America.
Library of Congress Catalog Card Number 72–172883

Foreword

In the dry, hot summer of 1212, Europe witnessed an event that is now remembered almost solely by its name—the Children's Crusade. The chronicles of the time mention it only in passing, and historians ever since generally have dismissed the subject in a footnote. Steven Runciman's authoritative, three-volume *History of the Crusades,* for example, devotes only five pages to the Children's Crusade, and yet it was one of the most extraordinary events in an extraordinary time.

At the beginning of the thirteenth century the rulers of Europe had lost their enthusiasm for attempts to recapture Jerusalem from the Moslems. Four major efforts had already ended in failure. Despite this, Pope Innocent III sent his bishops throughout Europe in an attempt to organize a fifth crusade before the hard-pressed Christian strongholds in the Middle East slipped back into Moslem hands. Ignored by kings and nobles, Innocent's appeal somehow reached a shepherd boy, no more than twelve years old, known only as Stephen of Cloyes. Stephen believed he had been asked by Christ Himself to lead a crusade of children who would recapture Jerusalem not by defeating the Moslems, but by converting them.

Stephen began preaching in the town of Saint-Denis, a religious center that attracted pilgrims from all over France. His message quickly spread and that summer three separate armies of children set out for the Holy Land from France and Germany. They had so little notion of the world that some of them would ask, as they approached towns on their way to the Mediterranean, "Is that Jerusalem?" A terrible drought afflicted Europe that summer and their route took them through districts which were near famine. Much of the continent was still wilderness, the roads were primitive, and the people were not always friendly. The sufferings of the children were terrible, and many died along the way.

Stephen had assured his followers that the Mediterranean would open before them so that they might walk to Jerusalem. When this failed to happen, most of those who had joined the crusade decided to turn back, but some were determined to go on. Remnants of the two armies from Germany got as far as Brindisi at the foot of Italy, before finally giving up. At Marseilles, the army of French children led by Stephen was offered passage to the Holy Land by two local merchants. Perhaps five thousand accepted the offer and set sail. Nothing more was heard of them until eighteen years later, when a priest who had sailed with the children reappeared in Europe with word of their unhappy fate. At that point they disappear from history utterly.

In the eight centuries since Stephen preached, the Children's Crusade has presented historical problems deserving closer study than they generally have received. The main question is, what happened? Since the crusade was so clearly doomed to failure, chroniclers of the thirteenth century tended to assume that Stephen had been prompted not by Christ but by the devil. The Reverend George Zabriskie Gray, a level-headed nineteenth-century clergyman who had little patience for the superstition he associated with "popery," described the crusade as a "delusion," by which he meant something modern psychologists would probably call mass hysteria. It would be hard to deny that the children were deluded, but this fails to explain why so many committed themselves so completely to so hopeless a task. One must remember that they expected to succeed, and that, assuming the truth of what they had been taught, there was reason for their optimism. The medieval church certainly believed that God could part the waters of the Mediterranean if He desired to do so. No one doubted that God took a close interest in the contest of Christendom with the Moslem world, and the Church often prescribed a pilgrimage, or participation in a crusade, as the best way to end an evil in the everyday world, such as drought, famine, infertility, or chronic illness. Common sense might say that Stephen's plan was absurd, but the medieval church, taken literally, did not.

The Children's Crusade certainly had its pathological aspects, but it is better understood, I think, as a kind of litmus test for the sincerity of medieval religious faith. The children who set out for Jerusalem took their teachers at their word. They put their trust in God and expected to win by faith what their elders had failed to win by arms. Innocent claimed that nothing was more pressing than reconquest of the Holy Sepulchre; the children believed him. The Church said they would more than regain in the next world what they might lose in this; the children were accordingly ready to make any sacrifice. In short, they accepted literally what their elders, when it came down to it, had intended only metaphorically. During the nearly four centuries of repeated forays to the East, the Children's Crusade stands out for its religious passion and purity. They went armed with faith, where others went armed with steel, and they went for God, where others went for money, land, and power. "These boys shame us," Innocent is supposed to have said, "for, while they rush to the discovery of the Holy Land, we sleep."

Innocent's words were often echoed by Americans during the early 1960s when students went South to fight for civil rights, and later in the decade when they actively opposed the war in Vietnam. The sit-ins, the freedom rides, the voter registration projects, the teach-ins on the war, the demonstrations, the draft resistance, even the McCarthy campaign in 1968, were all infused with the moral intensity of a crusade and to a large degree were conceived and undertaken by the young. The Children's Crusade was a single, coherent event that blossomed and died within a year, while the American movement sprawled confusingly over a decade. Nevertheless, the parallels between the two events are not only that both involved the young and that both were in the name of ideals which their elders were more inclined to profess than to practice. In both cases, also, the young set off with an unshakable faith in the rightness of their cause and a conviction that the strength of their commitment was enough to overcome all difficulties. In both cases they aimed at completing business left unfinished by their elders. And in both cases they knew little of the past.

There is something infectious about the confidence of the young, and something exhilarating about their moral clarity. As a result, those who watch sympathetically from the sidelines sometimes fail to notice how harshly the world can treat those who have ignored history. The special poignance of the Children's Crusade lies in the fact that those who took part paid such a high price for their innocence. They were cruelly abused by Christians and Moslems alike, and the survivors were often both disillusioned and corrupted. Gray alludes to the number of young girls who fell or were sold into prostitution along the route of march, and of the young boys who turned to thievery and worse. The bands of children who tried to make their way back to France and Germany were treated with anger and suspicion and it is apparent they were no longer the innocents who had set out only a few brief months before. Of the nearly 100,000 children who joined the crusade at its beginning, Gray estimates at least a third never returned home.

This is perhaps the bitterest parallel of all with the movement of the 1960s. Young Americans did not experience nearly so hard a fate as the children of the crusade, but they still paid a high price for their idealism. They were not thanked for pointing out injustice in America, or for trying to stop a war that threatened to escalate out of control. The lives of thousands were disrupted, many went to jail or into exile, and a few were even killed or driven into hiding. Children who ran away from home looking for a new way of life in rural communes, or in the hippie ghettoes of New York and San Francisco, often found a brutal world of drugs, disease, and violence. More than a few simply disappeared.

None of those who took part in the movement escaped the effects of its ultimate failure. The passionate intensity of the young quickly burns itself out; when the process is ended, there is often very little left. It is by no means impossible that the activist generation of the sixties will be followed by a new period of apathy even deeper than that which preceded it. Like the Children's Crusade, the movement of the 1960s ended bitterly, demonstrating again, for those who had forgotten, that the world reserves no especial mercy for those who bring to it the highest hopes or the purest faith.

In his brief book the Reverend Gray brought together all the widely scattered accounts of the Children's Crusade. In some ways it was a surprising book for him to have written. His only other works, long forgotten, are a collection of lectures and a treatise on marriage. A practical, liberal-minded man, he nevertheless found his imagination aroused by the moral enthusiasm that touched the children of Europe in the thirteenth century. He was fascinated that so huge an event could have been so totally forgotten. Gray himself could never have succumbed to such a movement, and yet he felt keenly the poignance of the children's eager belief and the harsh fate to which it led them. Nothing has been learned in the last century which alters the story Gray told in 1870. The only difference is that it no longer seems quite so strange.

THOMAS POWERS

Southbury, Connecticut
September, 1971

Rubr. Hic vide perigrinacionem puerorum et
   qualiter per incantaciones sunt decepti.
Illis temporibus stupendum quid crevit.
Mundoque mirabilis truffa inolevit.
Nam sub boni specie malum sic succrevit.
Arte quidem magica ista late sevit.
Rubr. Hic est carmen quod ubique cantabatur.
Nycolaus famulus Christi transfretabit.
Et cum innocentibus Ierusalem intrabit.
Mare siccis pedibus securus calcabit.
Juvenes et virgines caste copulabit.
Ad honorem Domini tanta perpetrabit.
Quod pax jubilacio Deo laus sonabit.
Paganos et perfidos omnes baptizabit.
Omnis in Jerusalem carmen hoc cantabit.
Pax nunc christicolis Christus proximabit.
Et redemptos sanguine mire collustrabit.
Nycolai pueros omnes coronabit.
Rubr. Talis devocio ante hec non est audita.
Aures cunctis pruriunt virgines ornantur.
Annos infra sedecim evangelizantur.
Concurrentes pueri certant ut sequantur.
Et rumare viderant casso consolantur.
Ungarus Theutunicus Francus sociantur.
Boemus Lombardicus Brittoque conantur.
Flandria Vestfalia omnes federantur.

Friso cum Norwagia cuncti conglobantur.
Prurit pes et oculus pueros venantur.
Illi de Brundusio virgines stuprantur.
Et in arcum pessimum passim venumdantur.
Risum luctus occopat digne lamentantur.
Plorant matres ut Rachel nati morti dantur.
Vanitates hauriunt pueri fraudantur.

Anon. Chron. Rhythmicum

Here you will learn of the long wanderings of boys and how they were
deceived through charms and imprecations.
It is amazing what they believed in those times.
And the staggering slaughter that grew out of it throughout the land.
For to such fine youth great evil did befall.
Indeed they were lured away with secret magic art.

Here is a song that was sung everywhere:
"Nicholas chosen by Christ will be transfixed
And he will travel to Jerusalem with the innocents.
Fearless, he will tread upon the sea with dry feet.
Young men and women will unite chastely.
For the honor of God, Nicholas will perform great deeds.
What peace and praise will resound to a jubilant God!
Pagans and infidels will all be baptized.
Everyone will sing this song in Jerusalem.
Christ will proclaim peace now to Christians.
And His light will shine wonderfully on those redeemed in blood.
And He will crown the boys of Nicholas."

Such dedication had never been heard of before this.
All ears were astounded that young girls were included.
Those who were converted were under sixteen years of age.
Boys traveling together contended that they might follow.
And they raised such loud cries that it was useless to comfort them.
Children from all over France and Germany joined together in this
undertaking.

All the children were brought together by Friso the Norwegian.
He mutilated the eyes and feet of the boys who were sold.
The maidens were defiled in Brindisi
And sold far and wide to the most evil money grubbers.
The crying children whom he seized with jeering laughter were justly
mourned.
Mothers wept that the daughters born to them were given to death.
The fruitless venture of the children who were deceived drew mighty
sighs.

Preface

There are some minor episodes of history that have not received the attention which they seem to merit. Historians have been too much occupied with events of greater importance to stop and explore these byways as they passed them. The same reason led the chroniclers of the times to preserve no more than scanty details concerning them, and consequently these worthies often dismiss with a few words incidents that have more interest than others to which they give many a dreary page.

This has been the case with the transaction to which this volume is devoted. Although pertaining to a sphere so interesting as the child-life of other and remote days, yet it has been almost forgotten. Many are not aware of its occurrence. Some have regarded it as a myth.

It is generally referred to, with varying fullness, in works that treat of the Crusades but not always with accuracy of statement. The most copious accounts are given in Raumer's *Geschichte der Hohenstaufen,* Herter's *Innocent III,* Menzel's *Deutschland,* Wilken's *Kreuzzüge,* Haken's *Gemälde der Kreuzzüge,* Sporschild's *Kreuzzüge, L'Esprit des Croisades,* by Mailly, *Histoire des Croisades,* by Michaud, *Influence des Croisades,* by Choiseul d'Aillecourt, Mill's *History of the Crusades,* and Hecker's *Child-pilgrimages.* Many authors, in whose writings we would expect some reference to the subject, are entirely silent concerning it.

But, otherwise than with the brevity necessary to a casual mention in the course of historical narratives, this theme has never been treated. As far as I can ascertain, it has never been the subject of a volume, nor have the original materials been thoroughly explored and exhausted. A small Sunday-school book was published several years ago, called *The Crusade of the Children,* but it was merely a brief fiction based upon the event.

It is therefore because the field was untrodden and because I thought that the story told in its completeness would possess interest that I have written this book.

As regards the chronicles that refer to the event, a list is given of all that have yet been found by others and by myself. For their trustworthiness, it is sufficient for me that such writers as Wilken, Herter, and Michaud rely fully upon their statements. In the notes I have not thought it necessary to give the particular source of each fact in the course of the narrative, but have only done so in the case of those of prominence or of those that are peculiar.

Hecker regards it and treats it as one of the "Epidemics of the Middle Ages" of which he writes. They who wish to view it in that light can consult his pages. It may seem to some that to regard it as such and to call it by such a name is to open the door for the admission into the list of diseases, of many transactions that the world has been wont to view, not in that way, but rather as the manifestations of the universal "epidemics" of human ignorance and folly.

I have sought to write in sympathy with the little ones whose fortunes are followed in this strange movement. It has been difficult to restrain feelings produced by a vivid realization of their chequered experiences. While I pored during several months over the story in quaint and dusty chronicles where even monkish Latin warms with its theme, it seemed as if the children's songs were in the air and their banners in the breeze.

I hope that the attractiveness which the theme has had in my eyes may not have caused me to overestimate too much the interest it may have for others and that they who read it may find in its perusal some of the pleasure which accompanied its composition.

G. Z. G.

TRINITY RECTORY, BERGEN POINT, N. J.,
May, 1870.

Contents

Foreword   5

Preface   13

Chronicles, etc., Consulted and Quoted   19

CHAPTER I
Introductory   23

CHAPTER II
The Rising in France   38

CHAPTER III
The Gathering of the German Children   59

CHAPTER IV
The Army of Nicholas   68

CHAPTER V
The Army with the Unknown Leader   92

CHAPTER VI
The Return of the German Children   101

CHAPTER VII
The Journey of the French Children   106

[17]

CHAPTER VIII
The Tidings From Beyond the Sea   130

CHAPTER IX
The Fate of the Leaders and of the Betrayers   157

CHAPTER X
Ecclesia Novorum Innocentium   163

Appendices   169

Concerning George Zabriskie Gray   175

Chronicles, etc., Consulted
and Quoted

1. *Caffari, Annales Genuenses, ab anno* 1101. Annals of Genoa, by Caffari, a statesman of the time. To be found in Muratori's collection of chronicles, called "Rerum Italicarum Scriptores."
2. *Sicardi, Episcopi Cremonensis Chronicon.* The Chronicle of Sicardi, Bishop of Cremona. Also in Muratori's collection.
3. *Godefridi Monachi Sancti Pantaleonis apud Coloniam Agrippinam annales, ab anno* 1162 *ad annum* 1237. The annals of Godfrey, Monk of St. Pantaleon in Cologne. Found in the collection called "Rerum Germanicarum Scriptores," edited by Struve.
4. *Alberti Abbatis Stadensis Chronicon a condita orbe usque ad annum Christi* 1256. Chronicle of Albert, Abbot of Stade, from the Creation to A.D. 1256. Also in "Rerum Germ. Scriptores."
5. *Chronicon Cœnobii Mortui Maris.* Chronicle of the Monastery of the Dead Sea, from A.D. 1113 to A.D. 1235. Found in "Recueil des Historiens des Gaules et de la France."
6. *Anon. Chron. Rhythmicum.* Anonymous Rhythmical Chronicle. In Rauch's "Rerum Austriacarum Scriptores." Probably written by Jo. Benedictus Gentilotus.
7. *Roger Bacon, Opus Majus.*
8. *Chron. Alberici Monachi Trium Fontium Leodinensis Dijocesis.* Chronicle of Alberic, Monk of Liège. Found in the "Accessiones Historicæ" of Leibnitius, Vol. ii.
9. *Roger de Wendover's Chronicle,* commonly identified with that of *Matthew of Paris,* of which it is a sequel.
10. *Fragment by an unknown author, prefixed to the Chronicle "Alberti Argentinensis,"* found in the collection of Christian-Urstisius, called "Germaniæ Historici Illustres."
11. *Chron. anon. Laudunense.* Anonymous Chronicle of Laon. Found in "Recueil des Historiens des Gaules et de la France."

12. *Bibliotheca Mundi, Vincentii Burgundi Præsulis Bellovacensis,* etc. Library of the World, by Vincent, Bishop of Beauvais. Vol. iv., which is called *Speculum Historiale.*

13. *Chron. Sythiense Sancti Bertini.* Chronicle of St. Bertin, by Jean d'Ypres. In "Recueil des Historiens des Gaules et de la France."

14. *Chron. Sancti Medardi Suessuonis.* Chronicle of St. Medard's Monastery at Soissons.

15. *Lamberti Parvi, Leodinensis Sancti Jacobi Monasterii Monachi Chron.* Chronicle of Lambert of Liège continued by another monk, *Rainer,* by whose name it is often called. Found in the collection compiled by Edmund Martin and Ursinus Durand, called "Veterum Scriptorum Monumentorum, historicorum, dogmaticorum, moralium amplissima collectio."

16. *Gesta Trevirorum,* in same collection.

17. *Thoma Cantipratani, Bonum universale de Apibus.* Thomas of Champré.

18. *Ogerii Panis Chronicon.* Chronicle of Ogerius. In Muratori's collection.

19. *Petri Bizari, Senatus Populique Genuensis Historia.* History of Senate and People of Genoa, by Peter Bizarus.

20. *Magnum Chronicon Belgicum.* The Great Belgian Chronicle. Found in Pistori's Collection of German Writers.

21. *Fasciculus Temporum.* In the same collection.

22. *Gesta Dei per Francos.* Deeds of God by the French.

23. *Chronicon Argenteum.* The Silver Chronicle. In Muratori's collection.

24. *John Massey's Chronicle.*

25. *Anonymous Chronicle of Strasburg.*

26. *Uberti Folieti Chron.* Chronicle of Hubertus Folietus.

27. *Chron. Senoniense.* Chronicle of the Senones.

28. *Chronicon de Civitate Januense, ed. a Fratre Jacobo de Voragine.* Chronicle of Genoa, by James of Vorago, or Jacques de Vitry. In Muratori.

29. *Chron. Rotomagense.* Chronicle of Rouen.

30. *Anon. Chron. Austriacum.* Anonymous Austrian Chronicle.

At least the first six Chronicles are contemporaneous, that is, they contain information written by persons that lived at the time of the Children's Crusade. The others were compiled at later dates (nearly all within a short time after the event), and their value is due to the fact that their materials were drawn from other contemporaneous documents that now are either destroyed or else cannot be found.

As editions of these works vary, it is unnecessary to state the volumes or pages where reference is made to the Children's Crusade. It will be found by simply turning to the date of the transaction, as the Chronicles narrate the events of each year consecutively. I found many of the authorities in the Astor Library. Some of them I consulted in the Imperial Library in Paris. Several had never been explored.

Other authors whose names are given in the notes are writers who have, in recent times, treated of the Crusades or kindred subjects.

CHAPTER I

Introductory

I

The Holy Land! What manifold associations cluster around that little spot of earth on which break the blue waves of the Mediterranean when they reach its easternmost limit! Memories the most sacred, the most tender, and the most thrilling cause the very name to call up before us a vista of the past such as no other land possesses. As we muse on the sound of the words, we hear the singer's harp and the prophet's lyre, and we catch echoes of the apostle's eloquence; there rise up memories of men and women whose stories are the world's best treasure; the forms of Abraham, of Samuel, of David, and of Isaiah sweep by in majesty, and, after them, lovelier and loftier than all, we see the figure of that One for whom they looked. O, what a land is that which has felt the footsteps of Incarnate Deity!

What a history that land has seen of peace and of turmoil, of freedom and of bondage, of glory and of shame! Across it has the tide of conquest rolled in every age; its plains have been enriched by the blood of many a different race. It lies before us, as we think of it, now in the sunshine of the days when Ruth gleaned in its fields, now in the splendor of Solomon's rule, and then we see its condition portrayed in that medal which the Roman victors struck, where, at the foot of a lonely palm, a weeping maiden sits, and beneath which we read the mournful words: *Judea Capta.*

How many hearts have loved that land! Patriotism in its most ardent forms has never equaled the devotion that Israel's children have felt for Israel's soil. When within its borders, they have loved it with an intensity that made each hill a shrine, and the thought of leaving it like the thought of death. When absent from it, in their repeated exiles, their hearts have gone out to its mountains and its valleys, its skies and its streams, with yearnings that could not be expressed. Wherever they have sojourned, it has still been to them their only home, and today, in every clime, a scattered nation loves it of all lands alone. They dream of the promised time when it shall be their own abode again, and, when their lives are closing, they journey thither with tottering limbs, to die, because they think the sleep of the grave is sweeter there.

How many feet have sought that land! The pathways to it from every part of earth have been worn by the staves and the footsteps of pilgrims. In the front we see the venerable form of him who, "when he was called to go out into a place which he should after receive for an inheritance, obeyed, and he went out, not knowing whither he went." Thence, down to these busier times, stretches the long procession of those that have traveled far, to kneel and to dwell on soil that, to the pious heart, is like no other soil. And as it has been in the past, it will be in the future. Oldest shrines may be deserted, superstition may pass away, but the sense of reverence and the power of association will never so far perish that they who have the Bible will no longer care to visit the Holy Land.

Poets may tell us of romance, but there is no romance like that of this consecrated Palestine—consecrated by the lives that have illumined it, by the love that has been lavished on it, by the blood that has been shed for it, by the Voice that has been heard in it! What land is like that ancient Canaan, which, so fair and so cherished, has given us all a name for Heaven!

But of all the associations linked with that magic name, none are more strange than those of the wars for its liberation from the Moslem. The Crusades alone would endue any land with a deathless interest.

When the followers of the false Prophet had overcome its feeble defenders, pilgrims still sought Palestine, undeterred by the perils they might meet. But as years passed by, they were more and more oppressed and maltreated, so that they who returned brought back to Europe sad tales of suffering of the believers there and of increasing desecration of the spots connected with the life and the passion of Immanuel. At length, in the eleventh century, these reports became so numerous and so exciting that there ran throughout Christendom a thrill of indignation. Then Peter the Hermit raised his voice to plead for the deliverance of those sacred scenes, and the response came from every nation of Europe. Thus began those wonderful wars, in which, with a devotion and persistency that are unique in history, host after host assembled, fought, and died. Even as the billows of the sea roll, one after another, against a rocky coast, so did the noblest and best of Europe's life, for more than two hundred years, rush against the exhaustless ranks of Asiatic power, and as vainly. At times success seemed near at hand, but the heathen front rolled back the tide and stood defiant and unmoved at last.

It is with an episode in this war of ages that we are now to be concerned. We are to tell how, in this mighty movement, there was a wave of child-life, to describe the part in that undying love for the Holy Land and in the weary seeking of its shores, that has been taken by children's hearts and by children's feet.

But before entering upon the theme, it would be well to prepare the way by glancing at certain points that suggest themselves, and, first of all, let us review the history of the Crusades, in order that we may perceive the causes which led to the arousing of the young to interest themselves in the struggle—

To chase these pagans in those holy fields,
Over whose acres walk'd those blessed feet,
Which *eighteen* hundred years ago were nail'd
For our advantage to the bitter cross.

II

State of the Cause of the Crusades

During eighty-eight years Palestine had been in the hands of the Crusaders, and Christian kings had ruled in Jerusalem. But this episode of romance and of glory was ended when, in 1187, Saladin routed the Christian armies at Tiberias, after which all the land was subdued, save a few strongholds over which there still rose the banner of the Crusaders. This catastrophe awakened grief and consternation throughout Europe, and at once the third Crusade was undertaken by the Germans under Barbarossa and the English under Coeur de Lion. The exploits of the two allied armies revived for a while the drooping hopes of the Christians, but soon there arose perfidy at home and treason in the camp. These did as much to render fruitless the achievements of Richard as did the power and skill of Saladin. Consequently, at the end of the campaign the Crescent waved as defiantly as ever over the land of Israel.

The fourth Crusade from 1195 to 1198 led by Henry VI of Germany was equally a failure. There were gained some brilliant victories, but dissensions divided the armies, and at last a truce was made with the Mohammedans. It is true that these victories made the Crusaders masters of the seacoast, but, when the armies departed, the Christian king found himself in possession of cities which he was unable to garrison, and which he felt could be held only by the sufferance of the enemy.

The fifth Crusade, preached in 1198, was perverted by the avarice of Venice and the ambition of its leaders, to the conquest of Constantinople. The knights, plunged in the luxury of that city, heeded not the appeals from Palestine but allowed the besieged and suffering, for whose rescue they had enlisted, to linger and die without an effort in their behalf. Fortress after fortress was wrested from the Christians, until at length there remained to the king, John of Brienne, but the city of Ptolemais; while to the north, only Tripoli and Antioch owned the sway of their counts. The Sultan was preparing a vast army with which these feeble forces would soon be overcome. Then, moved to desperation by the emergency, the Christians sent to Europe a heartrending cry for help.

But Europe responded sluggishly to the appeal. It was not until several years after the ordering of the sixth Crusade by Innocent that an army departed for the scene of conflict.

It was during this interval that the movement of the young occurred, they having been aroused by the measures taken by the Pope to excite the people.

For these measures were varied as the energy of the man would lead us to expect and resulted in a feverish excitement throughout Europe. He wrote to the sultans of Cairo and Damascus, urging them to yield the contested land. But his other efforts were of a more practical nature. Priests and bishops were sent everywhere, to awaken enthusiasm by appeals, arguments, and threats, repeating often: "I came not to bring peace, but a sword." Processions were held in the cities and towns, to entreat God for the imperiled cause and to enkindle the zeal of the beholders. Sermons had no other theme. The Savior was spoken of as a king banished from his heritage, and Jerusalem as a captive queen, appealing to the loyal heart to enlist in her behalf. Salvation was almost made to depend upon the recovery of the Holy Sepulchre, and, in dwelling on the scenes of the Savior's sufferings, the true vale of those sufferings was forgotten. Innocent himself, in his uncompromising zeal, revoked permission to engage in all other Crusades, except that against the Albigenses, and endeavored to stop all wars, so that nations might concentrate their energies upon this great enterprise. He crowned his labors and appeals with his famous exclamation, "Sword, sword, start from the scabbard and sharpen thyself to kill!"

As so many disastrous and fruitless expeditions had dampened the interest of Christendom and shaken its faith in the Crusades, little response was given to the frantic efforts of the Pope; but the arts and appeals which had so slight effect upon the people kindled the ardor of the young and made them zealous for the cause to which their elders seemed indifferent. They had not known the calamitous issues of so many similar undertakings; it was new to them, and not an old, sad story. The flaming descriptions of the Holy Land, vivid references to its associations, the favor of God which attended its defenders, and the glory of fighting in its behalf aroused them to become victims of a fate more sad than that of others who sought to free it, as it was more touching.

But their adventures have been passed over with little notice. Amidst the din of the contending armies of Crusaders and the clash of steel, few have heard the footsteps and the songs of three armies of youthful and unarmed combatants, who made their little effort for the holy cause. Although they did not win great victories or enduring renown, yet it may be that their story will interest us as much as that of the more hardy soldiers.

We are now to collect and narrate such details of that story as have been saved from oblivion, and, as we begin, it is with regret that they are so few. Withdrawing our attention from the conflicts of princes and of sultans, let us listen for a while to the part taken by the children in that weary struggle which has been aptly called the "World's Debate."

III

Contemporaneous Events

The thirteenth century opened in Europe amidst bloodshed and confusion, and over many lands there hung the lurid clouds of war. All the troubles of that troubled era were due to one moving spirit, who called himself the vicegerent of the Prince of Peace, but who, under the impulses of ambition and revenge, acted rather as if the Vicar of the Prince of War. Innocent III, surnamed "the Great," the most arrogant of popes, assumed the tiara in 1198 and soon had embroiled all Europe in conflicts of different kinds.

Passing in review the various lands, there comes first before us Germany, whose Emperor Otho IV possessed a character that rendered it improbable that he could treat the many vexed questions of jurisdiction over the petty states of Italy without clashing with so unyielding a rival as Innocent. New jealousies grew rapidly between them, besides those inherited with their respective positions, until, in 1210, the Emperor was solemnly excommunicated, and to the thunders of the Church was added the more serious declaration of a war without mercy. The Pope selected as his champion young Frederick, called "of Sicily," son of the Emperor Henry IV, and promised him that if he could wrest the crown from Otho, he should wear it as his own and occupy the throne by whose steps he had been reared. Otho replied by the ban of the empire against the pretender, a weapon only second to excommunication, and, in 1211, there began a cruel war, waged with skill on either side, that ended in 1216 when the former combatant died and Frederick succeeded to the empire to commence his splendid reign, the most brilliant one of the Middle Ages.

In England, we find John on the throne. He had been king since 1199, and was a monarch little inclined to bear with the pretensions of the Pope, but as little fitted to oppose them. In 1206, the storm broke, when an issue was made on the appointment, by Innocent, of Stephen Langton to be Archbishop of Canterbury. This the King resisted, claiming that the Primate should be chosen in England. He declared in a rage that no other should ever enter the country. In 1208, Innocent excommunicated him, and John was added to the motley list of those who have fallen under the displeasure of the Bishops of Rome, and who have been subjects of a document so eminently Christian and merciful as their ban. The King held out well for a while, as the national feeling was on his side, but at length the suspension of all religious rites produced their effect in the discontent of the people. When to this was added the preparation by Philip of France to conquer the land which the Pope had given him, John was obliged to submit, and to consent to hold his realm as a vassal of Rome.

As to France, it was to a great extent a scene of combat. Philip, seeing his opportunity in the weakness of the King of England, resolved to endeavor to expel all foreign rule from the land, and to put an end to the anomaly of large parts of his realm being really the domains of John. He prosecuted the task with vigor and success, and, in the opening decade of the century, had regained many a province that had long been a jewel in the English crown.

But there were other troubles and wars than these. It was an era of Crusades, for no less than three were commanded by Innocent at the opening of this century. They were directed, not against dwellers in Asia or Africa, but against inhabitants of Europe, for now the name was applied to all wars in which the Pope was interested. Two of them were against heathen. In Eastern Europe there was one preached against the Prussians, excited chiefly by the monks, who found that their unbelieving neighbors would not be converted by their precept or example. As there were plunder and the Church's blessing to be won, as well as the glory of doing missionary work among idolaters, many flocked to the standard of the Cross, and soon rested, either in the homes they conquered, or (as we are to suppose) in the glory which the Pope promised to those who should fall in the conflict.

In the West, we find a Crusade against the Saracens in Spain, who had assumed so threatening an attitude as to alarm the Christians. These latter were divided among several petty states, which enterprising men who had conquered slices of land from the Moors had called kingdoms. The various rulers, appealing to Christendom for aid, prepared to strike a concerted blow. Innocent did all that he could for them. He sent letters to France, urging the bishops to raise soldiers for the cause, and held processions in Rome. A large number of knights crossed the Pyrenees and joined the army that was assembling under the king of Castile. After a brief campaign, on the sixteenth of July, 1212, on the plains of Tolosa, the power of the Saracens was broken in a desperate battle.

In a certain sense these two wars were really Crusades against the heathen, but that to which we now turn was a war against the Cross, and in no sense a Crusade. It will ever be accounted one of the greatest crimes upon the pages of history and in the career of the Church that prosecuted it.

It is unnecessary to detail the horrors of the persecution of the Albigenses. A brief statement will suffice.

In 1208, a Crusade was ordered against Raymond, count of Toulouse, for venturing to protect his subjects who rejected the yoke of Rome. The energy of the Pope's measures and the prospect of plundering for Christ's sake that which was then the fairest and the richest district of Europe soon gathered an army of great size. Under the skilful leadership of Simon de Montfort, called "the General of the Holy Ghost," a coarse and brutal wretch, the Crusaders won victory after victory. All captives were put to death, in accordance with Innocent's command, who, when asked how to tell heretic from catholic, replied: "Slay all; the Lord will know his own!" It is a joy to think how true this was, as we read of the sufferings of these humble martyrs. Finally, the battle of Muret, in 1213, put an end to all organized resistance on the part of the Albigenses, and the "banner of the Cross" waved in victory over a devastated land. Their swords reeking with the blood of women and children, and their tents full of stolen riches, these exemplary followers of this "General of the Holy Ghost" from their orgies and their revels sent to the Pope the pleasant news that false religion and immorality had been extirpated. How nearly connected, sometimes, are tragedy and comedy!

Such were the wars and transactions of the era in which occurred the incident that we are to describe. But what was the condition of the people? Let us briefly answer this question, that one may know the state of the lands whence the children issued, and the influences which surrounded them in their homes.

IV

The Condition of the People

This was such as might be expected from the character of the times when war and turmoil seemed everywhere supreme. Vast districts were desolated and their inhabitants sighed and starved, while in others that armies had not ravaged, the people lived in daily dread of pillage. Society was disorganized and law a mockery, for the peasant had from it no protection, and the baron held it in defiance, so that the former, unless some lord was interested in preserving him for his own plundering, was at the mercy of any of the fierce outlaws who called themselves nobles. The only shelter for the lowly was the Church; the only fields that were not pillaged were those her officials owned. Nearly all Europe was in this condition; the exempted regions were few, and most of these were only safe because too poor to devastate. Tormented and wearied, millions prayed in agony and want, for peace or death.

Such a state of affairs naturally resulted in ignorance, as great as the prevailing poverty. In the midst of such distractions there was little chance for study, and anyone who could read or write, unless an ecclesiastic, was regarded as a wizard, while many of the clergy themselves would not have been able by either test to prove their position. There was not, perhaps, a darker era during the ages of gloom, as regards misery and ignorance, than this beginning of the thirteenth century. Life must have been a burden, and men little better informed than the brutes, with which they tilled their fields for precarious crops.

As may easily be imagined, religion was at a low ebb, and while armies were fighting for the Cross, few knew the teachings of that emblem. The instruction which the people generally received from those appointed to minister in holy things was a system of absurd superstitions, wherein they learned of deeds of questionable saints and supposititious martyrs, and the honor due to God was rendered to a woman, enthroned in his place.

To illustrate the state of affairs and show the example set by the clergy in France where the Children's Crusade originated, with which we are to be concerned, let us describe two customs, or ceremonies, of regular occurrence, and they will help to realize the extent of the prevailing ignorance concerning pure and undefiled religion. The first of these was called the "Feast of the Fools." [1] It was observed, not only in Paris, but in many other parts of the land, in the cathedral cities. In the former place it occurred on the Feast of the Circumcision, in others on Epiphany, and, in a few, on Innocents' Day, whence it was also called the "Feast of the Innocents." On the appointed day the priests and clerks met and chose an archbishop and a bishop from among their number. They then proceeded to the cathedral, led by the mock prelates, arrayed in great pomp, and after entering the edifice, began orgies of the most sacrilegious character. Masked, and dressed in skins of animals, disguised as buffoons, and even in the garments of

[1] Du Cange.

women, they danced and jumped about, shouting blasphemous exclamations and obscenest songs. They used the altar as a table, and during the performance of mass by the mock bishops, the others ate and drank around it, and played with dice. Exerting all their ingenuity to devise desecrations of the place, they burned the leather of their old sandals as incense, and crowned all by defiling the church, in postures and acts of unmentionable indecency. It seems as if this were giving vent to that which they felt during the whole year, that religion was a fable, and their duties the acts of a play. Eudes de Sully endeavored to suppress this sacrilege, but in vain. We find it still practiced a century later.

The other custom which shows the degradation of the Church was that called the "Feast of the Asses." [1] Although as general as the former, it was most popular in the south of France. The proceedings in Beauvais were as follows: The people and the clergy chose the prettiest girl of the town, and, placing a beautiful babe in her arms, mounted her on a richly caparisoned ass to represent Mary and the Savior. In great state she was led from the cathedral, where the selection had been made, to the parish church of St. Stephen, which the procession entered. The maiden and child, still on the ass, were placed on the gospel (or north) side of the altar, and the mass was commenced. Whenever the choir ended the Introit, the Kyrie, the Creed, or any other part which was chanted, they added a chorus, consisting of the sounds, "Hin-ham, Hin-ham," which were uttered so as to represent as nearly as possible the braying of the animal. A priest preached a sermon in mingled French and Latin, devoted to the exposition of the good qualities of the ass, and at the end repeated a hymn [2] composed of a bar-

---

[1] Celebrated January 14.

[2] It being a curious relic, the entire hymn sung on this occasion is added here. It is found in Du Cange's *Glossarium Novum,* etc., where the ceremony is described.

barous mixture of the two languages, whose every stanza was
followed by a refrain which may be thus translated:

> O Sir Ass, why do you bray?
> Why with that beautiful voice do you scold?
> You shall soon have plenty of hay,
> And of oats, much more than can be told.

When the whole profane farce was over, the officiating
priest, in dismissing the congregation, said, instead of "Ite,
missa est," "Hin-ham! Hin-ham! Hin-ham!" The people, as
they dispersed, replied with the same sounds, repeated three
times, instead of "Deo gratias."

HYMN TO THE ASS

Orientis partibus
Adventavit asinus
Pulcher et fortissimus,
Sarcinis aptissimus.

The sun shines on the ass
Most beautiful and brave
As he approaches
Bearing his burden most properly.

Chorus:
  Hez, sire asnes, car chantez?
  Belle bouche réchignez?

  Vous aurez du foin assez,
  Et de l'avoine à plantez.

Chorus:
  O Sir Ass, why do you bray?
  Why with that beautiful voice do you
    scold?
  You shall soon have plenty of hay
  And of oats much more than can be
    told.

Lentus erat pedibus,
Nisi foret baculus,
Et eum in clunibus
Pungeret aculeus.

Slow were his feet,
As if he needed a cane,
And they jeered at him
For his clumsiness.

Chorus.
  Hic in collibus Sichem,
  Jam nutritus sub Ruben:
  Transiit per Jordanem,
  Saliit in Bethlehem.

Chorus.
  Here in peaceful Sichem,
  Already nourished by Ruben,
  He travels through Jordan
  And leaps toward Bethlehem.

Chorus.
  Ecce magnis auribus,
  Subjugalis filius,
  Asinus egregius,
  Asinorum dominus.

Chorus.
  Behold his magnificent ears,
  The obedient son,
  The excellent ass,
  The master of all asses.

These things occurred in the most Christian land of Europe, in the days of a pope who gloried in his zeal for Christianity, without encountering any rebuke from king or pontiff! What must have been the religious teachings of a clergy, so degraded, and so defiant of all things sacred! What ideas must the people have had of the Gospel, when their guides knew so little.

These few facts and hints are all that can be given, in view of our limits, to show what were the times, what the state of

---

Chorus.
Saltu vincit hinnulos,
Damas et capreolos;
Super dromedarios
Velox Medianeos.

Chorus.
Aurum de Arabia,
Thus et myrrhum de Saba,
Tulit in ecclesia
Virtus asinaria.

Chorus.
Dum trahit vehicula
Multa cum sarcinula,
Illius mandibula,
Dura terit pabula.

Chorus.
Cum aristis hordeum
Comedit et carduum:
Triticum e paleâ,
Segregat in areâ.

Chorus.
Amen dicas, asine,
   (*Hic genuflectebatur*)
Jam satur de gramine:
Amen, Amen, itera,
Aspernare vetera.

Chorus:
Hez va! hez va! hez va hez!
Biax sire asnes car allez?
Belle bouche car chantez?

Chorus.
He surpasses the fawn with his dance,
A fallow deer, a roebuck,
He is greater than the camels,
This swift magician.

Chorus.
Gold from Arabia,
Incense and myrrh from Saba,
The virtuous ass
Brings in wonder.

Chorus.
While he pulls the cart
With its many bundles,
This burden of heavy fodder
He drags.

Chorus.
He eats barley
And prickly thistles:
He separates the wheat from the chaff
In the courtyard.

Chorus.
Amen, Oh holy ass
   (*here they genuflect*)
Now full of grain:
Amen, Amen, now be on your way,
You despised beast of burden.

Chorus.
Oh, go! Oh, go! Oh, go, Oh!
Sir Ass, why do you go?
With that beautiful voice why do you
   bray?

the people, and what the events transpiring when, in 1212,[1] that episode occurred, which is now to be described. In Spain, the armies of Christians and Moslems are gathering for the great battle. Frederick is marshaling his adherents to conquer a crown. The Albigenses are falling in martyrdom, and John is defying the Pope. Gladly do we leave the transactions in the sphere of the rulers of earth to follow the fortunes of a movement among the lowly and the young.

[1] As regards the date of the Children's Crusade, there is some discrepancy among the chroniclers, but there is no doubt that it occurred in 1212, as all contemporaries assert, as well as the *Chron. Argent., Chron. of Laon,* and Ogerius Panis. The variations are the following: *Chron S. Medardi* gives as the date, 1209; Thomas de Champré, 1213; John Massey, 1210. An error in the existing MSS. of Jacques de Vitry reads 1222 for 1212. But the authority of contemporaries should be conclusive, as the historians Michaud, Hecker, Wilken, and Raumer are agreed.

CHAPTER II

The Rising in France

I

Cloyes and Its Hero

Through that part of the old province of Orleannais which is now called the Department of Eure-et-Loir, and which is a vast, chalky plain almost denuded of verdure, there runs the little river Loir, in a southerly direction, until it joins the beautiful Loire, which on its course to the sea flows past gray old cities and famous châteaux. About twenty miles west of Orleans the valley of the former river widens, and in this basin, between the hills, surrounded by smiling meadows, is the town of Cloyes that has one association in a history of centuries to endue it with interest. Although more ancient than many other places in the vicinity, it has yet slumbered through the ages in obscurity, its cares and traditions and characteristics having been handed down undisturbed through generations which witnessed many changes elsewhere. Recently a railway has been constructed, which runs near the town, and its loud whistle sounds through the little streets, as trains pass the station on the plateau above.

It is an ordinary French village, with its square marketplace, where are sold wooden shoes, fruit, crockery, and the other miscellaneous articles peculiar to such a scene; its *Mairie;* with the imperial escutcheon at present hanging where so many other similar pictures have swung; its dirty shops and staring houses, and its dilapidated church, whose pictures and images might be thought to render idolatry impossible, because they

come up to none of the requisites of the second commandment
in regard to resembling anything "in the heavens above, in the
earth beneath, or in the waters under the earth." But still the
scene before one is attractive, as he stands on the old stone
bridge by which the main street crosses the Loir. The little
river comes from behind the trees of the park of an old château,
which is seen a mile distant. After lazily turning here and there
a mill wheel, when it reaches the precincts of the village, it
passes beneath our standing-place, to run through the green
meadows and beneath shady willows, until it enters the little
valley, by which it issues from this basin, where in some earlier
days it formed a lake. On the eastern side of us lies the village,
extending about a thousand feet to the declivity, which forms
the limit of the valley in that direction. On the other side of the
river, green fields extend about half a mile to the base of vine-
clad slopes.

This bridge is a pleasant place for musing on a summer
afternoon, and the scene recalls past days, for the country is
full of historical interest. Many a knight and soldier slept here
for the last time on the eve of the battle of Fretteval, where,
close at hand, Philip Augustus was defeated by Richard Coeur
de Lion, in 1194. And the people of this quiet hamlet were
awakened by enthusiasm, as was all that nation, when Jeanne
d'Arc passed through their streets on the way to seek Orleans
and to win for herself immortal renown.

It is in this village that our story begins.[1] For here in the last
years of the twelfth century or the first of the thirteenth was
born a boy who was named Stephen, probably after the saint
of his birthday, the twenty-sixth of December. Had it not been
for him, this place might never have been mentioned in history;

---

[1] There are various authorities for the fact that Cloyes was the birthplace and
home of Stephen. Among others, see the *Chron. Anon. of Laon,* which says he
was "ex villa Cloies, juxta castrum Vidocinum." Joh. Yperius says he was from
the diocese of Chârtres.

but his fame is forever linked with it, as the only name by which he is known is "Stephen of Cloyes."

His father was a shepherd, or a poor peasant, and Cloyes was then a miserable hamlet. The Loir ran by it then as now, but the banks which it washed, instead of being highly cultivated and densely peopled, were tilled to an extent only sufficient to feed the few inhabitants, who, in squalor and ignorance, knew little of luxury or of comfort. No hard and smooth highway led to the neighboring cities. The scanty traffic and the little travel had for their use a wretched and often impassable path.

Among such circumstances Stephen passed his infancy and began his childhood. When old enough to hold a staff and chase a refractory lamb, he was sent to be a shepherd boy, and he spent the summers upon the plains around his home, no better and no worse than others who led the same life, although, as his acts subsequently proved, mature beyond his years.

Obscurely and quietly his life glided away, until, in 1212, he became, as we are to see, the one upon whom was centered the attention of France.

We have already noticed the many means resorted to by the hierarchy to awaken the slumbering interest of the people in the shattered cause of the Crusades. Among these were frequent processions, when every expression of grief and of entreaty was called into use, to impress upon the beholders a feeling that God commanded them to enlist under the again uplifted banner and to arouse either their ardor or their fear.

There had long existed an ancient custom of the Church, observed on St. Mark's day, April 25th, called the "Litania Major," or Greater Litany.[1] It was a processional litany, instituted centuries before by Gregory the Great during the ravages

---

[1] See among others Joinville's *Memoirs of Louis IX* for description.

of the plague, but generally still maintained in Latin Christendom. On this day the altars were shrouded in black, and priests and people went through the streets of towns and cities, chanting prayers and carrying crosses likewise draped. From this last feature, the day was popularly called the "Black Crosses." At the time of which we are speaking, this ceremony was adapted to commemorate the sufferings of those who had died in the defense of the Holy Land, and to implore mercy in behalf of the Christians now beleaguered there, as well as of the many others who were pining in slavery. We can well imagine that such an observance, accompanied by stirring sermons and vivid threats and promises, would have excited the people, especially the young, who had neither the experience nor the judgment requisite to discern the hopelessness of the Crusades and the delusiveness of such appeals.

Stephen had of course heard of the desperate state to which the combatants of the Cross were reduced, and stray pilgrims and priests had told to the villagers of Cloyes stories of adventure and of glory which could not fail to excite his credulous mind. But all his ardor was redoubled when, in the neighboring city of Chârtres, he beheld the procession referred to above.[1] The black crosses, the loud and affecting litanies, the appeals which plead for an insulted Christ and his enslaved soldiers, the solemn ceremonials, the tears and emotions of the crowds worked upon him most powerfully and made him burn with desire to play a part in the expulsion of the hated Mohammedans from the land sanctified by the life of Jesus and hallowed by the possession of his tomb.

All alive with such emotions, he retraced, at evening, his homeward steps. And as he mused thereafter, in his loneliness on the hillside with his flocks, his imagination reveled in deeds of daring and in pictures of sacred scenes until he was ready

[1] Johannes Yperius.

for any enterprise, prepared to believe, with unquestioning credulity, any story, however wild and improbable.

While in this excited state, there appeared to him, one day, a stranger, who at first said that he was a returned pilgrim from Palestine on his way to a distant home and asked for some food. Stephen could refuse nothing to one who had been where he longed to be and had seen places for whose rescue he was ready to die. He only asked, in return, to be told of the wonders of the Orient and of the exploits of the brave heroes who had fallen there in battle, or who still lingered in the few remaining cities. Readily did the stranger comply with his request and tell him that which delighted his ears. Having thus gained an influence over the boy, he announced himself to be Jesus Christ, and proceeded to commission Stephen to preach a Crusade to the children, promising that, with him as their leader and prophet, they should win that victory which soldiers and nobles had failed to gain. He also gave the astonished youth a letter to the King of France, commanding that monarch to furnish aid to the new enterprise. Thereupon the pilgrim, undoubtedly a disguised priest who had heard of Stephen's enthusiasm and thought him a suitable instrument for the purpose of arousing the people, disappeared as mysteriously as he had come.[1] But he had played well his part, and rarely has a deception been so successful.

[1] The *Chron. Anon.* of Laon relates this interview of Stephen with Christ, and says that he showed, without any expression of doubt, the letter which the Savior gave him. I have adopted the explanation suggested by Sporschild and others, and which commends itself to reason, that Stephen was duped by some priest who found him ready to believe even such a thing, and ardent enough to assume such a charge. There must have been an incident of some kind to put it into the boy's head to undertake such a mission. Again, he certainly showed some letter as proof of his call, which he could never have written, nor anyone else in Cloyes; it was clearly the work of an ecclesiastic, which confirms the above theory. And if in the nineteenth century, the people of France believe that the Virgin appeared at La Salette with a babe in her arms, they would much more readily have believed in the thirteenth century that Christ appeared in person, when it was to effect an end considered so intimately allied with his religion.

After this, to be a shepherd boy was no more possible to Stephen. Higher duties called him, he said, when rushing homeward, he told of his interview with the Lord to his bewildered parents and neighbors, and showed his celestial letter to the King. There was no reasoning with him. Carried away by high hopes and by the dignity of his supposed call, he entered at once upon his work. To all he narrated his story and to the welcoming ears of his companions he told that now, when the defenders of the Holy Sepulchre were few and their ranks thin from the ravages of disease and war, when man's plans had failed, God had revealed his plan, which was to give the possession of Palestine to the children who should enlist. "For the last time have we heard of defeat," cried he; "hereafter shall children show mailed warriors and proud barons how invincible are youths when God leads them!"

But the field was too narrow in Cloyes. From a point so obscure, he could not arouse France. Some more central place must be sought, and at once he fixed upon the great shrine of the land, the object of countless pilgrimages, where to ever changing crowds, he could preach his Crusade and spread to homes of every district the intelligence of his enterprise. He resolved to go to St. Denys.[1]

II

St. Denys

Five miles north of Paris is the city of St. Denys, the place of burial of the martyr Dionysius. He was one of the seven holy men who established churches in Gaul, and from whose labors resulted the conversion of the land. Dionysius founded the Church of Paris and was its first Bishop. In 272, under the reign of Valerian, he suffered martyrdom. In the fifth century a church was erected over his grave, around which a town sprang up, to which was given his name. From the time of Dagobert,

[1] *Anon. Chronicle* of Laon.

all the kings, and many other members of the royal family were buried there, so that it became the central point of France and identified with its interests. Here, too, was kept the sacred Oriflamme, or the holy standard of the realm, which originally was the flag of the Church but was committed to the King as its guardian, when he went to fight enemies of the nation, and as such, was venerated by Saint Louis and inspirited the Maid of Orleans. The royal standard had previously been the cloak of Saint Martin, but the Oriflamme superseded it and became the symbol of the honor and existence of the kingdom.

The monks and priests who were interested in rendering the place attractive soon made it a center of pilgrimage and succeeded in impressing it upon the people that great were the benefits of a visit to the tomb of the saint. Legends without number were fabricated. He himself was said to be Dionysius the Areopagite, for which there was not a shadow of evidence, and a marvelous series of events were strung together and called his life. Of all these fictions, the wildest which is still taught and believed was that concerning his death. It was said that after very cruel treatment he was beheaded and his body thrown into the Seine, but that, issuing from that river, he carried his head in his hands for the distance of two miles, to the place where he desired to be interred.[1]

Of course the grave of so eminent a saint was soon a great resort for those who thought that he who could do so much for himself might do something for them. Pilgrims continued to increase in numbers, until it became, like the tomb of Saint James at Compostello in Spain, a national shrine, whither came thousands for physical relief and mental consolation; perhaps, sometimes, for spiritual aid.

[1] It was concerning this that Ninon de l'Enclos, when asked if she believed that the saint carried his head all the way, said: "La distance ne vaut rien. Ce n'est que le premier pas qui coûte."

In the commencement of the thirteenth century the influence of the shrine was at its height, for wars and Crusades could not deter the people from seeking its presence.

To St. Denys, then, do we behold Stephen of Cloyes journeying in the month of May, 1212. Dressed in his shepherd's attire, his crook in hand, and a little wallet by his side, he departed from the obscurity of his home and of his infancy. With bounding heart and exuberant hopes, he walked in eagerness which ignored fatigue. As he went, he preached his mission in the towns and cities by the way. But even Chârtres and Paris could not delay him long for he was in haste to reach the place which was to be the scene of his glorious labors. At last he arrived there, and everywhere, by the door of the church which contained the tomb, in the marketplace, and at all hours to astonished audiences he proclaimed the new Crusade.

Gifted with extraordinary powers of speech, he succeeded in enchaining the attention and gaining the admiring reverence of his hearers. To an enthusiast this was an easy task, with a subject so suggestive and in such a place. He told the old story of the sufferings of the Christians in the Holy Land and of their languishing in slavery, and the audience seemed to hear the clank of their chains as the speaker dwelt on their cries for help. And not only were their breasts stirred by that appeal, they also were told of the state of their brethren who were besieged in the few cities which they still held, and their hardships were a fruitful theme.

But Stephen had a still more powerful argument and a more potent appeal. He pointed to the sepulchre of St. Denys, thronged by its worshipers, and then contrasted its condition with that of the sepulchre of the Savior. The one was guarded by believers and the scene of unrestrained devotion, the other insulted by the presence of infidels and receiving not a prayer from those who would love to worship there. He then asked them if they would tolerate this, if they would not strive to make the Savior's tomb as honored and as free from defilement as the Saint's.

He showed the letter to the King, to confirm the doubting, and asked if Christ's commands were to be disregarded. He repeated the narrative of his interview with the Lord, and, to add credibility to his authorization to be the prophet of the new Crusade, told many incidents of a supernatural kind. He said that when he returned from his visit to see the procession held to implore God's mercy for the cause of the Crusades, before he had been commissioned by the Lord, he went to the pasture grounds of his flocks and found them absent. After searching, he discovered them in a field of grain. Enraged, he began to drive them thence with blows, when they all fell on their knees and begged his forgiveness. This, with other signs, said he, led him to believe that great things were in store for him, even before he had been visited by Christ.

He soon became the saint of the day, and the shrine was abandoned to listen to his stirring words. Especially was this the case because he worked miracles. It is said that he healed the sick and made other supernatural signs bear witness to his authority.[1] They who were credulous enough to come to St. Denys and to believe the legends which made the place what it was would not be apt to discredit the claims and the miracles of Stephen.

But especially was enthusiasm aroused in the young who visited the place or who were brought thither by their elders. The call of Stephen appealed to natural feelings, and they gladly believed him when he said that for them was reserved all the glory of the rescue of the Holy Sepulchre.

Accordingly, as the pilgrims departed from St. Denys, they bore to their different homes the story of the new apostle, the

[1] Vincent de Beauvais.

successor of Peter the Hermit, and of Bernard. The children
rejoiced in being the exclusive recipients of God's lofty commission and told their companions of the eloquence and the
power of Stephen. Alive with emulation to play a prominent
part in the enterprise, they commenced to seek adherents. The
matter spread like a contagion. As there were in the audiences
of Stephen pilgrims from all parts of France, soon in every
region of the land was his mission known, and children were
excited to dreams of terrestrial fame and celestial glory. The
movement began, regardless of feuds of rulers, of difference
of government, or of wars. It spread in Brittany, where the
English ruled, as well as in Normandy, recently added to the
domains of Philip; in Aquitaine and Auvergne, likewise just
freed from the sway of the foreigners, as well as in Provence,
where the king of Aragon was sovereign; in Toulouse, red with
the blood of martyrs, as well as in peaceful Gascony. The
children knew not, or cared not, what rule their elders acknowledged and were not interested in the wars for power. The
undercurrent of their life was untouched by the storms which
disturbed the surface. Consequently, while the adults were prevented from unity of action and from yielding to any interest
in the Crusades which they may have felt, by the commotions
and the political divisions of the land, the young were one,
and, regardless of tongue or of state, responded to the appeal,
from the Channel or the Pyrenees, from the Rhône or the
Loire. The voice of Stephen found everywhere a ready echo,
and when there went among them those who sought to enlist
adherents, they had an easy task. All the children united in
saying exultingly, "Long enough have you, knights and warriors, so boastful and so honored, been making your fruitless
attempts to rescue the tomb of Christ! God can wait no longer!
He is tired of your vain, puny efforts! Stand back and let us,
whom you despise, carry out his commission! He who calls can
insure the victory, and we will show you what children can do!"

III
The Minor Prophets

An old chronicler, while describing the events of these times, dwells at length upon the excitement caused in some parts of France by the frantic appeals and by the arts of the clergy in their endeavors to awaken among the lower classes that interest in Palestine which slumbered among the upper ranks of society. He also gives many signs which the Lord sent to add to the power of the emissaries of the Pope and tells us many a curious and wild story in this connection. Among these he says that "it is affirmed for a certainty, that every ten years fishes, frogs, butterflies, and birds proceeded likewise according to their kinds and seasons; and at that time so great a multitude of fishes was caught that all men greatly wondered. And certain old and decayed men affirm, as a certain thing, that from different parts of France an innumerable multitude of dogs were gathered together, at the town of Champagne which is called Manshymer. But those dogs, having divided into two parties and fighting bravely against each other, nearly all slew one another in the mutual slaughter and very few returned home." [1] Such, says he, were among the wonderful incidents which accompanied the commencement of the Children's Crusade, and, added to the prevalent excitement, made the children ready to believe that their call to rescue Palestine was the great event which those signs were intended to herald.

As has been said, the more enterprising among the youths who had listened to Stephen returned home resolved to play a part in the coming episode of glory, only subordinate to "The Prophet," as he was called. Everywhere there arose children of ten years, and some even as young as eight, who claimed to be prophets also, sent by Stephen in the name of God. They went throughout their respective districts, eagerly appealing to

[1] *Chron. St. Médard.*

their companions to assume the Cross. They took as their text and their authorization the passage of Scripture which they interpreted to refer peculiarly to this undertaking: "Out of the mouths of babes and sucklings hast thou ordained strength, because of thine enemies, that thou mightest still the enemy and the avenger." It would have been difficult for the adult Crusaders to find a text as appropriate.

These "minor prophets" (as the chronicles call them) also claimed to work miracles and thus added to their authority and the effect of their preaching. Among the many who thus took it upon themselves to extend Stephen's call, the names of none have been preserved, except one. He was an adult, and, had he not risen to prominence on another occasion, his name would also have been forgotten. It was Jacob of Hungary, whose strange life, one of the strangest on record, will be traced at another time. In this movement he was active and was instrumental in arousing the northeastern part of France. The names and the careers of the many who made the mountains and valleys of the land echo with their discourses and their delusive promises are lost in oblivion.

When they had gathered sufficient numbers, they formed them into regular and solemn processions and marched through the towns and villages with circumstances of display in order to gain more recruits. Of course, in different districts, there was variety in their arrangements, and the details differed.[1] But, as a general thing, there was at the head of each procession a chosen youth, who bore the Oriflamme, a copy of that at St. Denys, and which was, like the colors of a regiment, an object of devotion, the symbol of honor. Many carried wax candles, some waved perfumed censers, while here and there were to be seen crosses borne aloft.

And as they marched they sang hymns, many of which were the creation of their fevered minds. Some were, however,

[1] *Chron. Rotom.* and *Chron. Mortui Maris.*

ancient, having been used in the previous Crusades, and having awakened the enthusiasm of thousands who slept on alien soil. But, in all the songs, the constant theme was that expressed in the frequently repeated refrains: "Lord, restore Christendom!" "Lord, restore to us the true and holy Cross!" [1] They adopted the watchword which for two centuries had rung through Europe and had been sounded on a hundred battlefields in Asia, which had spurred to action many a victorious, as well as many a vanquished army, and which now brings before us, as we hear it, the whole drama of the Crusades. Crying "Dieu le volt!" these children threw aside all other obedience,[2] and considered that they acted under a higher than human law.

The excitement was not confined to the children of any particular class or rank. As would be expected, the greater number were of the peasant order, or, as one chronicler says in general terms, "they were all shepherds." [3] The ignorance of the world which resulted from their seclusion rendered these peculiarly liable to deception. They who had never passed the precincts of their parishes or cantons knew nothing of the hardships of war, the extent of this world, and the distance to Palestine, nor of the stern realities which were concealed by the glory and the glitter of the Crusades.

But we are also told that many noble youths, sons of counts and barons, joined the processions which they saw marching past their castellated homes. There were peculiar reasons why they were susceptible to the appeals of the prophets and were seized with desire to take part in the enterprise. They had, from their birth, associated with the knights and warriors who had won fame and honor in the Crusades. They had heard for years, as familiar themes of conversation, of the brilliant deeds

[1] Roger de Wendover.
[2] Godfrey; *Chron. St. Médard; Chron. Raineri.*
[3] Godfrey the monk.

of brave men, who themselves often narrated to them their feats at Ascalon or at Tiberias. They had also heard recalled most tenderly, as objects of envy, those who had fallen in the sacred cause. Accounts of the beauty of the East and of the richness of its scenes, descriptions of Jerusalem and of the Sepulchre had they again and again listened to, from those who had been in those wonderful places. It was unavoidable that influences such as these should have a mighty effect upon the young. It was natural that they would think and dream of the time when they might go in gorgeous armor, on prancing chargers, so to act that they too might be spoken of as were the many whose names were the household words of chivalry.

Again, there were those who had lost their fathers in the wars for the Cross, and they saw on the wall the sword and shield which reminded them that they were heirs of a noble fame. It would have been strange if such children were not fond of reveries and anticipations of glorious deeds in the same cause. Many had resolved that one day they would take those honored weapons, and, seeking the land hallowed by deathless memories, would complete the work of their sires, or else sleep by their side in the same consecrated earth.

Consequently, when such youths heard of the armies of children assembling at the summons of Christ to rescue Palestine, they felt that the time had come for the realization of their cherished dream.[1] And when from the hills whereon stood their homes they saw the processions pass with uplifted crosses and with banners waved by the breeze which bore to their ears inspiriting songs of triumph, they could not stay but hurried to join the throng, and either to assume positions as leaders, or as willingly to obey the orders of some once despised peasant. And so it happened that in the bands hurrying to Stephen was represented many a name that had been honored in the

---

[1] Lambert of Liège.

hosts of Godfrey and of Guiscard, of Louis VII, and of Thibaut.

Of course, the motives which led the young to join in these processions were not always the purest or the most religious. Many gladly embraced the opportunity to escape from the restraints of home and to secure freedom for their evil tempers and desires. To them this was not the golden chance to deliver the sepulchre of Christ; they cared not for its honor or for the sufferings of its champions—it was only the golden chance to gain a dreamed-of liberty from parental rule.

But we may not deny that the mass was stirred by feelings of a pious nature. To those in the tender years of childhood it was a touching tale, that of the grave of Jesus in the hands of heathen, and the recital of the sufferings endured in its behalf could not fail to impress them most strongly. All, therefore, who had any piety were as ready for this summons as tow for the spark, when urged to join in this new Crusade which was to be triumphant and bloodless, Christ himself having appeared and promised victory.

But we are told that many girls also joined the companies which traversed the land. Some statements seem to indicate that quite a large proportion were of this sex.[1] The same reasons which prompted many of the boys would influence them, and both inability to repel them and willingness to have their numbers as great as possible would induce the leaders to tolerate and encourage their accession.

And thus from their thousand homes they came, when in the marketplaces, at the crossroads, by the wayside, the youthful prophets preached their mission and pictured the glory of the cause as well as the certainty of its success. From the battlemented castle on the mountain, from the cheerless houses of the town beneath, and from the miserable mud hovels of the

---

[1] Rainer's *Chronicle.*

hamlet in the fields rushed the deluded children to swell the ranks of an army, from whose weary march few would return again to their homes.

But the excitement was not confined to the children. Men and women joined the assembling bands in no small numbers, prompted by a desire to rescue the Holy Land. They thought this appeal stronger than any other which had been made, and, while they were indifferent to the summons of priests, they listened eagerly to the call of the young prophets, thinking that they thus embarked upon a Crusade which had greater hopes and was to share a different fate from those whose disasters had desolated Europe. Even old age did not stand entirely aloof. Men of gray hair and of tottering steps were seized with the contagion, and in their second childhood imitated the ardor and credulity of that which had long since passed away.[1]

But many other men and women joined the armies from motives of a baser nature. All that were depraved in every sense found this a rare chance for profit. Abandoned women flocked in numbers in the expectation of fulfilling their infamous plans and of robbing as well as of ruining the youths. Thieves and sharpers never had such easy prey, and they did not neglect it. Everyone whose disposition would lead them to consider this an occasion for gain or plunder hurried to the rendezvous. Consequently there were introduced into the assembling troops of pilgrims elements which would necessarily work their demoralization, and we are not surprised when we find that that result ensued.

One may now see how motley was the composition of the numbers which the subordinates of Stephen gathered and led to him. Thus can we imagine the appearance of the bands which journeyed through the various districts containing boys and girls, nobles and peasants, old and young, men and women,

[1] *Chron. Dead Sea;* Rainer.

pious dupes and crafty thieves, praying pilgrims and vilest wretches.

IV
Opposition and its Results

It was not to be expected that such a movement could continue long without attracting the notice of the government. The king at this time was Philip Augustus, an unprincipled man and treacherous toward foreign nations but generally an able and a wise ruler of his own. His crimes against his allies, although he justified them on the plea of regaining his rights, resulted in the elevation of France, which at his death was united and strong.

When he first heard of the rising of the children, he seemed inclined to favor it, probably hoping that it might result in the arousing of the people to enlist in the Crusade and so enable him to obey the Pope, whom he was desirous to please that he might humiliate John of England, while at the same time it would save him the trouble of collecting an army for the purpose.

But the matter soon grew serious, and his counselors urged upon him that it was no temporary delusion of limited extent, but that the interests of the realm demanded its suppression, for not only would it carry away the youth to destruction but it would also produce confusion, disorder, and pillage. As Philip was endeavoring to reorganize and consolidate his kingdom, these representations succeeded in making him direct his attention to the movement. Yet it was a delicate thing to undertake to suppress a Crusade, although an affair of children. It might be really ordered by God, he reasoned, and the Pope might also take it under his protection and forbid all restraints upon it. It was a perplexing question, and therefore he referred it to the newly established University of Paris, that their wisdom might guide him.

After a consultation, in which they had to meet the fact that they might be accused of heresy, and where, in such an age of superstition, the natural advice would have been that given by Gamaliel to the Sanhedrin, the doctors gave the sensible reply that the movement should be stopped, and, if needed, vigorous measures should be used. Accordingly the King issued an edict, commanding the children to return to their homes and abandon the mad enterprise. Whether he had received the letter which Stephen showed, we are not told. If he had, he doubtless gave little heed to its alleged authorship, as from the Savior.

But his decree had little effect. The matter had gone too far to be arrested by a command. Few could be found who wished or who dared to enforce it and it was unnoticed, except by those who were influenced to obey it, or by others who were glad to have an excuse for leaving the assembling bands, being already homesick and weary.[1]

The King does not seem to have concerned himself any further about the affair, but in his many cares suffered his edict to remain unenforced. It may be that he was unable to carry it out, from want of instruments or from fear of the people. At any rate, the children continued to assemble unimpeded.

There were naturally other influences brought to bear upon the young to restrain them. Parents who had not been carried away by the frenzy did not like to see their sons and daughters running to unknown dangers and hardships. Their reason as well as their affection moved them to interfere. Yet persuasions, threats, and punishments were all as vain as had been the King's command. Bolts and bars could not hold the children. If shut up, they broke through doors and windows, and rushed, deaf to appeals of mothers and fathers, to take their places in the processions, which they saw passing by, whose crosses and banners, whose censers, songs, and shouts, and paraphernalia

[1] Concerning the King's conduct, see, among others, *Chron. of Laon.*

seemed, like the winds of torrid climates, to bear resistless infection. If the children were forcibly held and confined so that escape was impossible, they wept and mourned, and at last pined, as if the receding sounds carried away their hearts and their strength. It was necessary to release them, and saddened parents saw them exultingly depart, forgetting to say farewell. Regardless of the severance of tender ties, they ran to enlist in those deluded throngs that knew not whither they went.[1]

Opposition was also made by the faithful among the clergy. Knowing the certain issue of the scheme and having hearts unwilling to see the young overcome by inevitable disasters, they endeavored to check the excitement. But their efforts were also vain, for opposed to them were others, the crafty and un-principled priests, and the emissaries of the Pope, who rejoiced in the affair, because it was a means to excite the adults. Accordingly the cry of heresy was raised if any pious pastor used entreaty or earnest warning, and he was accused of frustrating a holy cause. The people who believed in the delusion caught up the cry, and children adopted it, until opposition was silenced. In this way, between the designs of those who were to gain by the movement, the superstition of the masses, and the enthu-siasm of the children, there was enough to overcome all efforts to arrest the daily increasing excitement.

The serious and right-minded among the people were at a loss to understand so unprecedented a phenomenon and en-deavored to account for it in various ways. The generally re-ceived belief was that it was the result of magic, the devil's agency, the cause assigned for all remarkable and inexplicable events in these ages. To this did the University of Paris attribute it, and more than one chronicler quietly says, as a matter be-yond question, that Satan was the author and guide of the affair.

But among the many stories invented to account for the

---

[1] Roger de Wendover and Rainer.

event is one that, although beyond all probability, yet is so strange that it deserves a passing notice, illustrating as it does the sentiment of the times.

It is said by one chronicler, who believed it, that many held that the "old man of the mountain" had liberated two enslaved clerks, and sent them to France to bring back an army of children, as the price of their liberty, and that these had originated the present undertaking.

This mysterious personage was the chief of the Assassins, who dwelt in an impregnable castle on a mountain in Syria. This sect of Mohammedans flourished for a short time, and they were the terror of the world, on account of their wonderful devotion to their master, who hired them out to those desiring their services, and, in the execution of whose orders, treachery was praiseworthy, danger was despised, and slaughter their habitual practice. The stealthiness and secrecy of their proceedings, and their remorseless thirst for blood, have caused their name to be adopted as the appellation of deliberate murderers. In order to secure such servants, who were called *Arsacidae,* the chief trained them from infancy, by an education wherein every emotion of a tender nature was stifled and fear of disgrace and of death obliterated. For such purposes, it was said, did he wish some children of France, and the hosts which were assembling were to be his prey. The horror in which the people stood of this man led them to believe the story. It is curious and awakens memories of our own days of childish credulity to find that the reigning "old man of the mountain" at this time was the famous Aladdin, the story of whose wonderful lamp is told in the "Arabian Nights." [1]

Still the movement went on, reproved by a few, applauded by many, variously regarded as the work of God or of Satan. Through the cities and hamlets, by the Seine and the Garonne,

[1] Vincent de Beauvais explains the movement in this way, and Jourdain thinks it not improbable.

were seen the bands, marching with their banners, singing their songs, and telling how they were "going to God and to get the Cross in Holy Palestine."

As they passed by, the laborers left the fields and the artisans the shops; all business was suspended, and they who did not join their numbers crowded to see them, in curiosity or in admiration. They were housed and fed for nought. Many gave this aid from kindness, others from sympathy in the enterprise, while few dared deny to such numbers any request which they might make. And so, before long, the various prophets could send word to Stephen that they would bring a vast army for him to command and to lead.

But, as the nature of the narrative requires that we follow the order of time, we now leave France in the ferment of the gathering and turn to describe events which transpired in Germany. These we will trace to their end and then return to Stephen and his followers.

CHAPTER III

The Gathering of the German Children

The tidings of the preaching of Stephen and of his celestial mission were quickly carried eastward, and pilgrims returning from St. Denys told of him in Burgundy and Champagne, where the story spread to the lands along the Rhine. The people here had been subject to the same attempts to arouse them to interest in the Crusades which the French had experienced, and were as ready for the new delusion when it came, thanks to the activity of the papal emissaries with their litanies and their addresses.

In a village near Cologne, whose name has not been recorded, there lived a boy who was to be the apostle of this Crusade in Germany, and play the part which Stephen acted in France. He was born in about the year 1200,[1] and had been familiar with the prevailing excitement from his infancy, so that now he was full of interest in the Crusades, and at once was seized with a desire to emulate the young prophet of Cloyes, when the fame of this latter reached his ears.

Nicholas, for we know no other name, is said to have been induced to assume the part of a prophet to preach the new Crusade by the influence of his father. It was not now a crafty priest, but a parent, who, knowing the precocity and the zeal of his son, saw that he would be a proper one to imitate the example of Stephen, and worked upon his young mind until the boy believed himself called by God to the task. The motive

---

[1] Sicardi says he was "a boy less than ten years old."

which influenced the father may have been a desire to see his child famous and great, that he might enjoy the reflected honor; or it may have been desire to profit by the event and to rob the deluded victims of his work. This latter prompting is the one that was ascribed to him by the people, for the old monk who saw all the progress of the affair tells us that he was "a very wicked man"; and the people of the region have left on record their opinion of his character in the summary vengeance that they meted out to him when the results of his work were apparent, as we will see at the close of the story.

Probably directed by his father, Nicholas went to Cologne and there preached his mission. There were the same reasons to recommend it as a suitable place for the purpose, which made St. Denys such for Stephen; it was a great national shrine.

Old Colonia had long been a great and influential city, but it rose into new prominence when, in 1162, it became the religious center of Germany. At that time its archbishop, Raynuldus, brought back as his share of the plunder from his clerical foray with Barbarossa to sack Milan, among other articles not mentioned, the bones of the "Three Kings of the East." The legend of these who came "with a great multitude of camels to worshippe Christ, then a little childe of thirteen dayes olde," is one of the most noted of the medieval myths. The history of these particular bones, whether those of the Magi or not, begins with their removal to Constantinople by Helena, who discovered so many valuable relics of a sacred nature. The Emperor Eustorgins took them from their shrine in Santa Sophia and gave them to the archbishop of Milan, from whence Raynuldus carried them to his city in patriotic zeal. For a while they reposed in a splendid shrine in the cathedral which Charlemagne had built, until the present grand edifice was constructed, where they still remain. From the very first there was great devotion paid to them, and the revered skeletons [1] listened as patiently to the supplications addressed

---

[1] It has been discovered that one skull is that of a child, having milk teeth.

by the Germans as they had to those which they had heard in
Italy or Byzantium, yielding as ready attention, in a forgiving
spirit, to those who had gained possession of them by war and
robbery as they had to those to whom they had been presented
as gifts. Rightly or wrongly won, relics always hear the prayers
of their *de facto* owners. This is a curious fact connected with
them.

In their common interest in this sacred place, the adherents
of Otho and of Frederick forgot their feuds and quarrels, so
that it was never more frequented than now when Nicholas
went thither to proclaim his call to the great work of rescuing
Palestine by children.

What we know of his labors there is told us by Godfrey,
an eyewitness, the compiler of a chronicle of that city. He was
a monk, one of those who passed their lives in quiet cloisters,
noting down events which transpired around them, illuminat-
ing missals, and praying venerable prayers.

According to his aggravatingly short record, Nicholas came
to Cologne and at once began to preach. He had, as had his
French brother, a story to tell of a supernaturally received
charge, which was readily believed, as a confirmation of his
claims on their attention. He said that as he was tending his
flocks in the field, he saw a cross of blazing light in the sky
and heard a voice which told him that it was the pledge of his
success in the holy war. His father had probably heard of the
history of Constantine, or it was related to him by some priest
who had found him a credulous tool.

Through the throngs that filled the city he moved, telling
what he was to do, or preaching from elevated stations to the
gaping pilgrims, who, having swallowed the story of the bones,
were ready for his lesser fable. The people and the children
had been familiar with the incendiary labors of the envoys of
Innocent, and the latter were as excited as those of France by
the scenes which appealed to their ignorant and unreasoning
minds. He therefore found the way paved for his success. The

scene was still more suggestive and appropriate for the theme
than even St. Denys had been. He could point to the shrine
of the Wise Men, glittering with gold and jewels and surrounded by precious votive offerings of undisturbed pilgrims;
and comparing this with the state of the sepulchre of that One,
to their connection with whose history these men owed all
their fame, ask if the children he saw as well as the adults
were not as ready as those of France to endeavor to rescue the
holier tomb from its ignominy, under the guidance of him
whom the Lord had chosen to lead his servants thither.

We can imagine the scene presented during these days of
the spring of 1212, when Nicholas was gathering his followers
and pleading his claims. We can see him by the door of the
old Byzantine cathedral, which disappeared soon after that date,
standing on a platform or on a pile of stones, addressing the
crowds in motley attire who came to worship, and whose many
quaint dialects and curious dresses represented the different
regions whence they had journeyed. They listened eagerly as
he spoke and discussed among themselves the new wonder.
What stories were related of similar prodigies which had been
the theme of local pride in many a remote village! What de-
bates as to the probabilities of the success of this new prophet!
What expressions of hope that this might solve the mystery
which hung over the fate of many friends who had been
hurried away to the wars at the command of the baron who
was their lord! What eager thanks to God for his interference
to end the cruel and hopeless struggle for the holy places! Thus
can we fancy the manifestation of the interest of the throngs
that our little boy, so precocious and enthusiastic, addressed.
Among them we see old Godfrey moving, in his brown robe
and sandals. He has come out to see how this restless, turbulent
world is getting on, whose turmoil does not reach the seclusion and stagnation of the cloisters of St. Pantaleon, and is
noting down in his mind the strange things he sees, that he may

return to muse in his cell, or beneath some tree in the slumberous garden of the convent, upon the follies of men. At evening he will record, in his precious manuscript, along with the events of greater interest pertaining to the history of his peaceful asylum, what he deems worthy of mention among mundane affairs.

The oblivion which covers all these busy scenes is well represented by the change that has come over the shrine of the Wise Men, which is edifying to the traveler who visits Cologne today. A century or more ago, the shrine—a golden box of great value which contains the bones—was removed from the chief place in the cathedral to the eastern end, where, though more confined, there was room enough for the devotees who came in vastly diminished numbers to worship where hosts had once knelt. But as the "ages of faith" became more and more remote, the numbers lessened. The days of pilgrimage were ended, save for a few stragglers that still lingered in the rear of the vanished crowds. Fewer and fewer they became, until one day the last faithful, credulous soul, whom we would love if we knew him, knelt alone, solitarily told his beads in lowest murmur, asked some petition which came from a heavy heart, then rose and went away, uttering an "Amen" that closed the prolonged prayer of centuries.

The officials of the cathedral, wisely judging that the space might be better appropriated, and the remains be so arranged that the pilgrimages of curiosity, which took the place of those of piety, might be made profitable, moved the bones to a corner where they are kept in a room, to which admittance is gained, not by a prayer, but by a thaler. The writer not long ago examined the gorgeous casket in company with a number of nineteenth-century priests, who calmly and curiously talked of its carvings and adornments, and, without a genuflection, looked at the smooth skulls which the attendant exposed by opening a sliding panel.

But let us come back to Nicholas and other days. From Cologne the excitement spread, as from St. Denys, by means of those who sought their different homes. The extent of country, however, in which the children rose, was limited, owing to the prevailing dissensions of a civil nature, and because the Emperor found it a part of his policy to suppress the matter where he could, and thus thwart the Pope, as well as retain his people for his armies. Yet, within the limits of the vicinity of the Rhine and the neighboring land of Burgundy, the commotion was greater than in France, as is shown by the proportionately greater number that flocked to the Crusade.

Nicholas was aided by other youths, who acted as lieutenants and labored to gather adherents in their various districts, hoping to hold positions of rank. Of their names we have none preserved; so many other and higher sounding ones occupied the pens of the chroniclers that these were overlooked.

Very noticeable is one feature of the appeals which Nicholas and his assistants used. The triumph promised and expected was one of peace. The Holy Land was not to be won by battle nor restored to the Christian king by the slaughter of the Mohammedans, but the latter to be converted, and to accept, as believing subjects, the rule of the faith they had hated. In strange and touching contrast does this spirit stand out among the cruel and bloody memories of the time. It awakens a peculiar interest to read that when they marched from place to place, gathering adherents, their watchword was one so different from the barbarous and ruthless mottoes which expressed the temper of Crusaders, for they sang, "We go to get the Cross beyond the sea, and to baptize the Moslem infidels!" [1]

The excitement spread rapidly from town to town and from village to village, so that the bands which the "minor prophets" collected were rapidly recruited, and successively led to the

---

[1] *Gest. Trevirorum;* Godfrey and others.

rendezvous at Cologne. The mania increased daily and over-
came opposition. For opposition was made to those who would
follow the young preachers, but with the same results as in
France. Parents, friends, and pastors sought to restrain them
by force or appeal, but they whose hearts were set upon the
enterprise mourned and pined so, that we are told their lives
were frequently endangered as by disease, and it was necessary
to allow them to depart. Many hoped that at last, at Cologne,
the delusion would end, and various causes disperse the assemblage.

The composition of the gathering bands was as motley as
that of the companies that were collected for Stephen—probably more so. There were numbers of unprincipled creatures
that joined the ranks, led by various base motives, to gratify
their propensity to thieving or to lust, and all the refuse of the
region seems to have been drained, as we would naturally
expect. It was an opportunity for such persons that was too
good and too rare to be lost, and it was not lost. The number
of depraved women that mingled with the armies was, it is
told us, especially great, and to them is attributed the greater
part of the evils which ensued. The chroniclers refer frequently
to them and present a dark picture of the morals of the time.[1]
We can well imagine how the people dreaded the approach
of these bands. They not only feared lest their young would be
carried away by the infection, which no authority or ties could
overcome, but because with them came such a lawless, de-
moralizing rabble that would steal and rob with impunity.

Nevertheless, the vast majority were prompted by good,
though mistaken, motives. There were many reasons which
would lead multitudes to a sincere desire to liberate the sepulchre of the Savior and purify his tomb from pagan control,

[1] Jac. de Voragine says: "Multi autem inter eos erant filii nobilium, quos ipsi
etiam cum meretricibus destinarant." ("Many among them, however, were sons
of noblemen who yet were seized upon by harlots.")

and such as these were ready to undertake and to endure anything in order to promote that end. This swayed, undoubtedly, the mass of those children who persisted in the enterprise, while of course some were ruled by ambition or by desire for independence of the restraints of home.

With regard to the station of those who were gathered in the movement, there was great variety, all ranks being represented, led by promptings which appealed to each. There was a larger proportion of children of noble birth than was the case in France. Germany was always more alive to chivalrous excitement and her nobility more numerous. The country, particularly along the romantic Rhine, was studded with baronial halls, which were nurseries of daring and of knightly feeling. All the influences which would act on children of the lords to embark in this Crusade were thus especially potent, and there were more boys here than in France ready to go and combat the cruel Saracens, because a father or a brother had fallen at their hands. Thus the excitement ran through the upper class, and Cologne, the home of many noble families because a large and imperial city, is said to have lost so many children of rank and to have furnished so many scions on whom fair hopes were placed that the effects of the movement were felt for a long time after it had died away.

As to age, there were very many adults in the assembling crowds, as we gather from various statements of the chroniclers, and not only of those who joined them from lower motives, but many such were seized with the crusading spirit. They had become weary of the vain attempts to succeed in this terrible war, which had been made in the usual way; and this new plan at once was regarded by them as that devised by God, and destined to triumph, where, very evidently, ordinary warfare was not to achieve the result.

We are told, as an interesting feature which shows that some attempt was made at discipline, that a uniform was generally adopted.[1] It was an adaptation of the usual costume of pilgrims. They assumed a long coat, when possible, of a gray color, and upon the breast was sewn a cross, as customary with the Crusaders; for they claimed this character as well as that of pilgrims. This latter aspect was further enhanced by the carrying of a palmer's staff, and on their heads they wore broad-brimmed hats. There were many who but partially, if at all, adopted this costume, because they would not or could not procure it. Such a simple and quaint attire must have made a pleasing effect when a group marched by.

In this way was the region around Cologne kept in a state of ferment, as the bands continued to arrive at this central point, where Nicholas awaited them, until the time came for their departure for the Holy Land. Little over a month could have elapsed before the assembling was completed, and the various leaders had their recruits ready for the start, whether in the always crowded city, now doubly full, or in the towns and villages around. The greatness of the numbers collected in this brief period shows the enthusiasm of the movement. That it must have been so brief is seen from the fact that Stephen began his work in the spring; then the tidings spread to the Rhine. After this the gathering took place here, and these children marched to the Mediterranean; yet they reached that sea before the middle of August.

We now proceed to the next step in the prosecution of the Crusade, or pilgrimage. But here our narrative divides, for there was a division of the host assembled at Cologne, into two armies. The fate of that which started under the leadership of Nicholas will be first traced, and afterwards we will return to the fortunes of the other.

[1] Jac. de Voragine.

CHAPTER IV

The Army of Nicholas

I

To the Alps

One fair morning of June or July, in the year of grace 1212, our friend Godfrey, monk of St. Pantaleon, probably saw a strange scene, to which we have now come in the course of this narrative. Let us follow him out of the city, and witness with him what he beheld as the sun was gilding the towers of the churches, and still casting the long, westward-stretching shadows of early morning. Or, better, let us take our place on the walls, where we may stand, surrounded by eager crowds, and overlook the spectacle.

Upon the plain before us is a dense, waving concourse of people, who issue from streets and lanes by the open gates, or who come from neighboring villages by paths and roads bordered by hedges still glistening with the dew. All ages and both sexes are represented, and all are intent upon some important matter, as their motions and their murmurs tell. In the mingled sounds which come to us, we perceive at times the refrain of a song or the noise of altercation, while we hear also the lamentations of others whose gestures express great sorrow. As we watch the scene, a discrimination is in progress, and many join the forming ranks of an army whose insignia and banners become visible in regular array. At length all is ready. Nicholas takes his place as leader, and at a given signal the compact mass moves away, still followed by friends who would not cease to seek to arrest their beloved ones, and by the amazed eyes of the throngs upon the walls. Vain had been the efforts to stop the enterprise by parents, priests, and rulers. Too confident to be dissuaded, too reliant on their numbers to be intimidated, too elated to be discouraged, this band of twenty thousand children [1] commenced its march toward Palestine. We watch them from our station, as they recede, until behind some hill the procession disappears, and the sound of their songs and their shouts sinks into silence in the distance.

Their route lay along the Rhine. This region was not then, as now, densely peopled and rendered romantic by frequent, picturesque ruins. It was almost a wilderness then, with an occasional castle rising from lofty crags that bear at present but a shattered tower or crumbling walls. Upon the lordly Drachenfels, which stands as a sentinel at the portal of the valley of the Rhine, was the home of a wild baron, whose relics are now the peaceful loitering place of the tourist; and, as he saw the children wind across the fields, beyond the river, there arose in his mind pleasant thoughts of plunder. It was a subject of congratulation to the latter that the Rhine rolled between them and those grim walls. At Rolandseck was Roland's Tower, which then, as now, looked down upon Nonnenwerth's beautiful green isle cradled in the river. Gutenfels and Stahleck were the homes of rough men and fair women, to whom the lapse of centuries has given associations which are very poetical, but who found their daily life as real and as prosaic as we find our own. Rheinstein, from its vine-clad height, frowned down upon the winding river which soon disappeared in a gorge, where the superstitious boatman saw in every nook and crevice an abode of dragons or of sprites. Here dwelt then old Siegfried, whose name is linked with many a weird legend. And thus were some of the storied spots of this wonderful stream then marked by castles above or towers below; but, generally, the hillsides, at present so

[1] *Fasciculus Temporum.*

cultivated and whence come to the tourist the songs of "peasant girls with dark blue eyes," were covered with dense forests, where wandered the stags and boars, the wolves and bears, whose pursuit formed, besides war, the only amusement of these rude men of old.

As our children wander southward, let us seek to describe the manner of their march, and their experiences.

Of all the strange armies which those days of strange sights had witnessed, this was the most notable. There were no mailed soldiers, who marched beneath feudal banners that had waved over battlefields in Europe and in Asia; there were no chargers that carried strong warriors who held well-used swords; nor yet were there pilgrims of mature years, who had set out, unarmed, to pray in consecrated spots. It was an army of children, who were actually departing to recover possession of a land in whose behalf many a host had died in vain. In the van we see Nicholas, probably accompanied by an escort and attendants. Then the line stretches with varying regularity for several miles, and, over the uniformed ranks of little ones, rise the crosses and banners that are proudly carried. We see, among the numbers, the many adults who desired to share the glory of the enterprise or to plunder and corrupt. There were women who came to profit in their baseness or suffer in their weakness, and girls who were destined to a bitter lot of shame, instead of a rest in Palestine. And priests and monks were there, some to rob and some to pray. But the mass were boys of about twelve years of age.[1] They gave character to the army, and it is with them that we are concerned. They came from mansion and from hovel, from luxury and from want; the pedigree of princes was possessed by those who walked by the side of humble serfs.

As they marched along, they beguiled the time with narra-

[1] Sicardi.

tive and song. As to the former, there was among them a store
which was not soon exhausted.

The children from the castle told of knightly deeds by men
of famous names, and to the more credulous peasants repeated
what they had so often heard from their proud kindred, who
had won such fame in conflict. They who had never before
spoken with the despised boor, forgot their station, and wearied
not to answer questions concerning the life of the noble born,
which had been almost as sacred and revered in the cabins of
the lowly as the associations of the Holy Land. The serf-child
could only tell of obscurer feats of arms and of less exalted
deeds, which his kindred had known; but yet each was ready
to hear the wonderful stories of the other. In this way, throughout the host, the spirit of the cause was kept alive, and their
minds were inflamed into resolution to surpass the achievement
of squire, and knight, and baron. The fame of the heroes who
had fallen, to be immortal in song, or who had survived to
receive the love of woman and the envy of man was yet to pale
before the luster of the deeds of God's own army.

And songs, too, whiled away the tedious hours of wandering,
as well as aided in sustaining their spirits. Chroniclers expressly
say that singing formed a marked feature in their journey. They
sang many lyrics which returned pilgrims and warriors had
taught them, but which, it is sad to say, have been lost. They
also composed many of their own, which have shared the same
fate. It is natural to wish most earnestly that some of these
had survived, that we might learn something of the children's
feelings, and that we might enter into a fuller sympathy with
them, in reading the words that conveyed their emotions. But,
although we have not the language of these songs, we can
well imagine their themes. The constant subjects were the
restoration of the Holy Sepulchre and the glory of that triumph.
We need not labor much to realize the ardor which nerved
them to endure fatigue, when, their little hearts bounding with

excitement, they shouted in spirited tunes the expressions of the hopes and dreams of years.

From the oblivion of ages there has survived, however, only one of the hymns which were sung by them. It was brought by the recruits from Westphalia and had been sung by many a pilgrim before, on the way to Palestine. Its words and air, so well adapted to this present assemblage, made it popular, and it delights the Christian of today by the evidence which it affords that there lingered yet some appreciation of the truth of the Gospel, some love to the Savior. It seems as a gleam of light in the darkness of the age. Listen, then, children of the nineteenth century, to words that other children sang, as they marched along the Rhine, nearly eight hundred years ago.

Let us quote it first in the original, in which these little crusaders were wont to sing it, having modernized its antique German:

> Schönster Herr Jesus,
>   Herrscher aller Erden,
> Gottes und Maria Sohn;
>   Dich will ich heben,
>   Dich will ich erhen,
> Du, meiner Seele Freud' und Kron!

> Schön sind die Felder,
>   Noch schöner sind die Wälder,
> In der schönen Frühlingszeit;
>   Jesus ist schöner,
>   Jesus ist reiner,
> Der unser traurig Herz erfreut.

> Schön leuchtet die Sonne,
>   Noch schöner leuchtet der Monde,
> Und die Sternlein allzumal;
>   Jesus leuchtet schöner,
>   Jesus leuchtet reiner,
> Als all' die Engel im Himmelsaal.

TRANSLATION

Fairest Lord Jesus,
Ruler of all nature,
Thou of Mary and of God the Son!
Thee will I cherish,
Thee will I honor,
Thee my soul's glory, joy, and crown!

Fair are the meadows,
Fairer still the woodlands,
Robed in the blooming garb of spring:
Jesus is fairer,
Jesus is purer,
Who makes our saddened heart to sing.

Fair is the sunshine,
Fairer still the moonlight,
And the sparkling, starry host;
Jesus shines brighter,
Jesus shines purer,
Than all the angels heaven can boast.

How welcome is such a hymn from the past ages, and how it does add to our interest in these youths who used it! [1]

Thus singing their songs, they passed on southward, seeking Palestine. But it is natural to inquire if they did not know that the Mediterranean intervened; and if so, how did they expect to cross it? Did their leaders not have an answer ready for this question? We find, as a feature of curious interest, that they who had excited and promoted the Crusade had promised that the Lord would provide a pathway through that great sea to the land beyond its waters. Availing themselves of a home

[1] For an account of the discovery of this hymn, see *Evangelical Christendom* for May, 1850. This was a magazine formerly issued in London, and to its editors I am indebted for a copy. The hymn has since been published in various collections of sacred music in the above version, which is that made by the author of the article in the magazine referred to. Hecker aserts that it was used by the children.

argument, they pointed to the fearful drought which is recorded to have prevailed that summer, as evidence from Heaven that the army was to pass, like Israel's hosts, through the sea, for they said that the Mediterranean was drying up for this end. This was asserted in reply to the natural objections that there would not be enough vessels to carry such a vast number, or that, if they were obtained, the young pilgrims would lack money to pay for their transportation and their food. The story was believed, and the children were buoyed up and encouraged on the march by the anticipation of so signal an interference in their behalf. Surely, said they, if we are thus to triumph over the deep waters, as did the people of God in old times, we must win an equal success, and rest in the same land, by virtue of the same divine aid.

They journeyed onward through the domains of the lords and nobles who owed allegiance to France or to the Empire. Their fame may have preceded them, or it may not, yet their arrival was always the signal of commotion in every village, where they won new recruits from the astonished and enraptured children. Each member of the host told, in his own words, the same tale of a celestial call and of a certain success, and repeated, with embellishments of his own invention, the appeal in behalf of the defiled tomb of Christ. If night overtook them by any town or hamlet, they sought shelter where they could find it. One chronicler tells us that no city on the way could contain the army. Some slept in houses, where the kindhearted or the sympathizing invited them to rest; others reposed in the streets and marketplaces; while they who could find no space within lay down without the walls. But if, as was generally the case, the darkness found them in the open country, they passed the night in the barns and hovels, under the trees of the forest, or on the green bank of some stream, and the angel of sleep closed their heavy eyelids under the starlight. The day's march was wearisome to little ones who had never before been out of sight of home, and therefore they soon fell asleep, wherever it was. When morning came, they ate whatever they had in their wallets or what they begged or bought as they went. The line of march was again formed, the banners unfurled, the crosses uplifted, and, with the morning song they began another day of fatigue. At noon they rested by some brook to eat their scanty meal and quench their thirst, and again started to wander on through the quiet hours of afternoon, until the welcome sunset reminded them that they had passed another stage of their journey to distant—O, so distant!—Palestine.

But their great trials soon began. After what we have learned of the mingled elements in the army, it does not surprise us to learn that the evil-disposed spread every kind of misery, and that there ensued all sorts of demoralization. Those children who had any money were robbed or cheated of it, and they who had only food in their wallets soon had that stolen by the hangers-on and thieves. The depraved men and women gave way to their passions, so that vice grew daily, and parts of the camp became scenes of sin and lust. The disorders were increased by the rivalries of subordinate leaders, until at last they moved on, but little more than a loose, lawless concourse, without chiefs and without discipline. Consequently, they were at the mercy of those who for various reasons saw fit to molest them, and with impunity the wild barons could swoop down upon them from their fastnesses, and seize as many as they would, to hold them in harsh or basest servitude.

They reached at length the territory now called Switzerland, but which was then a conglomeration of petty lordships, most of them being subject to the Duke of Burgundy, but many belonging to the Emperor. Threading its beautiful valleys, and passing along its foaming rivers, they came to the shores of Lake Leman, and encamped by the walls of Geneva. Thence they sought the Alps, which rose grand and imposing before them. To cross those trackless heights was now the task to which the poor little children were to address themselves. Weary and worn, singing and sighing, they neared the blue mountains on whose summits rested the eternal snows.

II

The Passage of the Mont Cenis

Other causes than those already referred to had tended to diminish the numbers of the youthful army. As we hurry by railroad or steamboat through the regions they traversed, we have to exert our imagination to form an accurate picture of the condition of those lands at the date of which we are speaking. The population of Europe was very sparse, probably not one-tenth of its present amount, and it was generally restricted to the vicinity of cities. Tracts now thickly peopled and smiling with crops were uninhabited and untilled, and in them animals roamed unmolested. The few highways which led from city to city were wretched and devious, passing through dense forests, and by haunts of robbers who could, with no terror of law, plunder the unguarded traveler.

Journeying through countries such as those on the route which they followed, where population was scanty even for those times, produced terrible effects among the children. In fording streams where there were no bridges, many are said to have been drowned. We are also told that the wild beasts seized many an unwary or worn-out straggler. They often found themselves in these unpeopled regions without any food, and then they had nothing to eat but the wild fruit and berries by the wayside, so that starvation ended the lives of numbers, whose exhausted frames easily yielded to its pangs. Disease, produced by constantly recurring circumstances, tended also to thin the ranks. And from all these sorrows resulted the chief cause of the diminution of the army, which was desertion. Weary and discouraged, they fell away at every step and sought their homes in groups.

As far as can be ascertained, about one-half of the original number remained when they came in sight of the Alps, which rose before them peak beyond peak.

The route they selected was that over the Mont Cenis, which, in the Middle Ages, was the most frequented of all the passes into Italy. Into the heart of the mountains, then, the children plunged, where was a sparse population that tilled the valleys, and dwelt by the foaming torrents, gathering scanty crops from the little meadows which lay, here and there, between the streams and the rocks. But in these people our Crusaders found enemies instead of friends. For they were, we are told, to a great extent heathen and even idolaters, as were many of the inhabitants of the Alps up to this date, and the records of the time contain allusion to their constant depredations upon pilgrims and travelers. In the Valais there were numbers of Saracen Mohammedans, who had penetrated thither from the sea on forays and had remained, unable or unwilling to return.[1] Through these hostile ravines the army persevered until the ascent began in earnest. New trials now commenced, which rendered those of the past insignificant. The road was merely a narrow, stony path over streams and along precipices, over dreary mountain slopes, where grew only the heather and rhododendron, or over fields of unmelted snow.

The chronicles of the time abound in narratives of the perils encountered in the Alps, by those journeying, not for pleasure, but on various errands. There were merchants seeking their marts, soldiers seeking the battlefields or their homes, ecclesiastics passing to and from Rome. In view of the great amount of travel produced by the relations between the Pope and Northern Europe, by the pilgrim spirit that has long since almost died away, by the ceaseless plying of diplomacy, and by other causes peculiar to the Middle Ages, there is reason to

---

[1] Michaud's *Crusades.*

believe that the passes over the Alps were probably as much frequented then as they are now. Consequently the frequency of incidents of suffering was far greater when there were no roads as at present, but only rude bridle paths.

Among the most remarkable of all the passages on record was that of Henry IV, with his wife and child, when he was on his way to Canossa to humiliate himself before the Pope. His experience casts light on that of the children. His route was also over the Mont Cenis. Vast quantities of snow had fallen, and for several weeks no one had ventured to cross to or from Italy. At length the Emperor secured reluctant guides and started with many attendants. The ascent was toilsome and terrible. The Empress, with her babe, was dragged over the snow on oxhides, and wrapped in furs. The descent was still more perilous. The horses and mules were lowered from ledge to ledge, or else their feet were tied, and then they were suffered to slide down the icy slopes. Over the cliffs and precipices many a guide and servant fell, to be found no more. It was through such untold terrors and hardships that the subdued ruler of Germany passed to meet the stern presence of the Pope, his rival and his conqueror. Well has it been said that "he would be a hardy mountaineer, even now, who would undertake such a journey, unless a soul or an empire were at stake."

Many of the children who had not yielded under the past trials now felt they could do no more. The rocks cut their shoeless feet; the air of sunless chasms chilled them, while they saw that there was no hope of food or rest until the pass were traversed. Group after group then sadly turned their faces homeward, their ardor for the Sepulchre and the Land quenched by this revelation of what lay in the path by which they must be reached.

We may briefly follow, by the aid of scanty records and conjecture, the adventures of those who resolved to brave the passage. It lasted several days and nights, longer than usual, as they were disorganized, and their sufferings during this period surpassed powers of description.

The children of wealthy or noble families had been provided, we are told, with attendants who carried supplies of food and clothing, and thus were enabled to endure the hardships of the path. But as these cases were almost exceptional, there was little done in this way to lessen the trials of the mass. The others suffered severely from the want of food and in this state were entirely unequal to the exhausting labor of climbing difficult ascents. They had left home in the summer, when their raiment was thin; it had become scanty and ragged in the long and dusty march, so that they were exposed to the full severity of the cold. So they toiled on, hungry and tired, disheartened and discouraged by the gloomy mountain scenery, and by the ever new revelation of other heights beyond those they had thought the last. On through black forests of pines and firs, through moors, over ridges, leaping from stone to stone, as they met a stream, across treacherous snows into which they sank, and which froze their feet, and over jagged rocks which lacerated them, traveled this decimated band of children, which, a short month before, had departed from the walls of Cologne with exultant hearts and gleaming eyes.

No scene was more impressive and characteristic than that presented as they stopped to rest at evening. Glad, and yet sorrowful, to see the sun set, they ceased the weary walk, wherever the darkness overtook them. They ate the little bread that was left, drank of the thirst-provoking snow-water, and then, in their wet and ragged clothing, lay down upon the heather or the rocks. They who were so fortunate as to find any wood made a fire, around which they crowded for protection from the piercing cold that came in blasts from the gorges and glaciers above them. What pen can describe the emotions of those children, as they thus prepared to sleep, while they thought of their distant dear ones and of the comforts they had so wilfully abandoned!

What a sight did the Spirit of the Alps behold, as he saw these encampments, where, under the cold and solemn starlight or in the chilly rain, thousands of boys and girls lay sleeping, and, in dreams of home and of the Holy Land where they were to return in triumph, forgetting the trials of the day which had closed, and those to come with the morrow! How many fell into the sleep that knows no waking, and, when comrades rose to start in the morning, remained cold and stiff where they had dropped at evening! They could not be buried in the frozen earth; their bodies were left to molder away to dust.

At the summit of the pass of Mont Cenis there was, as there is still, a monastery where for four hundred years kind monks had dwelt, to furnish food to the pilgrims and travelers who had ventured on the journey unprovided or who needed somewhere to rest at night or a refuge from the storm. They also acted as missionaries to the heathen population around them and performed the necessary offices of religion for the Christians. Rejoiced must the young Crusaders have been to reach this hospice, which not only gave them food and partial shelter, but also reminded them that the worst of the journey was accomplished, the most dreaded obstacles surmounted, and that the exhausting ascent was now to be exchanged for descent.

After a brief stay, they passed on. As at length a turn in the path showed them the plains at the foot of the mountain, how the sight thrilled them! They saw the rivers, which looked like threads of silver through green fields of tapestry, and villages and vineyards that formed a scene of cultivation and of beauty unknown in their northern home. With renewed strength, they rushed downward until they trod the soil of Italy.

The present territory of Piedmont was, in those days, divided into many small states, independent and proud, but generally owing allegiance to the Duke of Savoy, or to the Marquis of Montserrat. Through these domains lay the path of the army, and it was a path of continued trial. They had hoped that, with the passage of the Alps, their sufferings would end; but they had now to endure trials of another nature. The Italians were embittered against the Germans, owing to the constant wars carried on by the Emperors, and, when these children were in their power, they visited upon them the sins of their fathers. They were subjected to cruelties of every sort. They were refused entrance to the towns; the lords seized many of them, whom they carried away to hold as slaves, disregarding the voice of the Church and of humanity. The army hurried from peril to peril, through a land to which they had looked forward so hopefully. At length they reached a mountain range, from whose summit they saw, in its beautiful amphitheater and facing its noble bay, Genoa "the proud." There was the sea, blue and boundless, which they had never beheld before, and, on the shore, bathed in the sunlight, lay a city which seemed a vision of fairyland to their eyes, accustomed only to the scanty splendor of Germany.

The effect of this sight can be easily imagined. The youngest and weariest were strong again, and the departed were pitied, as the goal of the journey lay before the crusading army. Banners which had been furled in despondency were raised again to float in the seaborn air. Crosses were again held aloft in exultation. Songs, which had not been heard for many a tearful day, were resumed, and hymns of triumph were shouted as hopefully as when they had been heard by the distant City of the Kings. Discords were forgotten. Nicholas, whose sway had been disregarded, was again their prophet and leader, and again were stories of triumph and of glory on every lip, and dreams of fame in every heart. No more Alps! No more wilderness! No more want, fatigue, and suffering! Only the path through the sea remains to be traversed, and then we will tread the shores of Palestine! Thus did the children exclaim, as they saw, from the hills where they stood, the towers and palaces of Genoa.

III

Genoa

On Saturday, the twenty-fifth day of August, in the year 1212, the army of children stood by the gates of Genoa, begging in the name of Christ and the Cross for admission, that they might rest after a journey of seven hundred miles.[1]

It was not such a band as had left the banks of the Rhine. Of the twenty thousand, only seven thousand remained under the guidance of Nicholas.[2] Where were the rest? They slept by every torrent, in every forest, on every hillside along the weary way. The route through Burgundy and Switzerland and over the mountain paths was marked by their graves or by their unburied corpses. Many had returned in sorrow to the homes they had left in enthusiasm, and others who had found new homes or had been kidnapped were never more to see, or to desire to see, the scenes of infancy. Only the most determined and robust were left, and as a consequence there stood by Genoa the flower of the youth of the Rhinelands, who had become rugged and strong, the weak and sickly having been sifted out by the experiences of the way. The same causes which had forced the feeble to relinquish the enterprise, or had exhausted them, had contributed to purge the band of the dissolute and depraved. Those who had enlisted merely with the desire to escape parental restraint and to indulge their sinful propensities would not be expected to endure the continued hardships, and, as soon as the attendant difficulties exceeded the gratification which they derived, they had turned their backs

---

[1] Ogerius Panis: "Die Sabbati, VIII. Kal. Sept." Vincent de Beauvais also gives this date.

[2] Sicardi and Ogerius Panis.

on the band, and either sought their homes readier to submit to rule, or else, as was the case with many, remained in the cities along the route, where they grew up in vilest habits, and where they swelled the ranks of the depraved. Likewise did the adults who had joined to plunder and to demoralize shrink from fatigue and seek other spheres for plying their arts, although not until they had worked great misery. In all respects, the army was therefore purified by its trials.

But very changed was the appearance of the seven thousand. Their garments were tattered and faded, their feet shoeless and wounded. Their faces had been burned by the sun and the snow, and their expressions saddened by sorrow. Yet they were capable of more endurance than they had been at first, and they were buoyed up by new confidence as they reached the shore of the Mediterranean.

Genoa was at this time at the height of her prosperity and shared with Venice and Pisa the commerce of Europe. Not yet had her decadence begun. It was to be a hundred years, before, in that long war, the Lion of St. Mark was to humble her; after that she had herself crushed her rival, Pisa. Now her port was filled with the shipping of all climes. Her merchant princes dwelt in palaces, many of which yet astonish the stranger. Her Senate surpassed in dignity all other governments, and the state of her Doges excelled in pomp that of the monarchs of Europe, whom they treated as equals. Many a score of galleys rode at anchor in her blue harbor, ready to avenge her insults and to preserve her colonies. Her territory extended far into the interior, for the Republic, though a city, owned wide domains, from whence came her soldiers and her food.

Before the august body which governed this state came the petition of Nicholas and his army that they might sleep within the walls but one night. They asked not to remain longer. They could not tarry, as they were in haste to reach the Holy

Land, to whose shores duty and desire impelled them. Nor did they ask for galleys, or for vessels of any kind, to transport them there. On the morrow, the sea which Genoa had failed to curb was to be divided by the Lord, and this army was to march dry-shod to the coast it sought. God had chosen that city as the place of this miracle, and the astonished Senators were warned, lest they refuse to aid those so signally under the care of Omnipotence.

The authorities heard the petition, and, in mingled wonder and pity, they considered it. But they did not hesitate long. Sympathy with the deluded youths moved them to consent that they might tarry six or seven days for rest and refreshment, for surely, said the Senators, they will return homeward when they discover their deception.

Eagerly did the boys receive the permission, and exultingly did they enter the city, where they anticipated enjoying such repose as they had not known since they had started from Cologne. They marched through the stately streets, regarding in amazement the sumptuousness visible on every hand, and thinking of the meanness of their own less favored homes. What a change was this from desert wilds and Alpine heights!

Their joy and wonder were equaled by the astonishment of the inhabitants, when they saw defiling through the gates and crowding the streets so many fair-haired children, who, carrying banners and crosses, sang in spirited songs their determination to rescue the Holy Sepulchre, to achieve that for which they had come from far beyond the Alps, under the guidance of a child. The merchant left his desk, the young ceased their play, the maidens gazed in wonder or in tenderness, the grave nobles were moved to surprise, as these blue-eyed youths from the Rhine passed by.

But, when once the permission to enter had been accorded by the Senate, they resolved on that same day to rescind it.

There were three reasons which were imperative.[1] In the first place there was to be feared the effect upon the morals of the city that might be produced by seven thousand unrestrained boys. In a short time they might, relying on their numbers, give way to lawlessness and introduce results which the jealous government well knew how to dread. Again, the Senate feared lest so sudden an addition to the population might produce a famine, for, situated as Genoa was, there was never any great superabundance of food. But the last and principal reason which weighed with the Senators was political. Emperor Otho was, as we have seen, at war with the Pope, and in the contest Genoa was ranged on the Guelph or papal side. This had been its party for many years, and the name of any German had become odious. The adults had learned to cherish this animosity in their experience of the rigor of the wars of Barbarossa, and the young had been trained to regard the coarse "Tedescas" as enemies of the Church, enemies of Italy, and as panting to lay hands on fair Genoa, as they had so ruthlessly done upon Milan. To shelter German children, then, although ostensibly on a Crusade, would be to harbor foes and to care for a hated race which the Pope had declared outlawed. Why might they not, the Genoese mob exclaimed, be emissaries of Otho, and endeavor to seize the city for him? But, more potent in the minds of the Senators than these fanatical cries of the populace was the consideration that Innocent might take it in bad part if they sheltered so many Germans, whose object, so absurd, might be doubted. To use a modern phrase, it would not give as clear a record as they wished. It might be used against them by some rival for the favor of the Pope.

The result of the deliberations was that the authorities told the children that they could only remain one night; on the

---

[1] For this action of the Senate, and the motives which ruled them, see Sicardi, Og. Panis, Petrus Bizarus, Ubert. Folietus, Jac. de Voragine.

morrow they must depart from the territory of the Republic. But, that mercy might not be denied them, exceptions would be made for those who should desire to remain permanently, and, giving up their wild scheme, promise to become good citizens. This was politic, for it might secure an infusion of strong and robust blood into the population, in which respect the hardy Northerners were the envy of the enervated dwellers in warmer lands.

The confident youths received the command in derision and laughed at the offer to give those who desired it a home. "We only ask to rest one night. Tomorrow you shall see how God cares for his army! Who would remain here, when there lies a path in the sea, between emerald walls, to the land where glory waits us?" Thus they cried as they prepared to sleep that night in the houses or in the streets, and with hopeful, proud thoughts they closed their eyes at evening.

The night passed away. In the morning, they rose to rush to the seashore and behold the new way upon its bed. But that sea rolled as yesterday; no miraculous chasm yawned to receive their eager footsteps. They looked in despair out upon the blue and sparkling waves, which danced in mockery, and learned at last how terribly they had been deceived. Hours wore away but brought no change. They then had to prepare, with disappointed hearts, to leave the city, and to deliberate upon the next step to be taken.

But the once derided offer of the Senate was not fruitless now. Many who had awakened to an appreciation of their deception, and who could not resist the argument of that undivided sea, resolved to remain in Genoa. They could not tear themselves away from the comforts of the city to encounter a renewal of hardships such as they had experienced. No, here would they stay, and, as well as they could, secure a luxurious home among scenes so different from their own abodes, which, if they could reach them, would now appear squalid and mean, in a cold land, where were no figs, no oranges, no vineyards. How many remained we are not told. It is stated by the chroniclers that there were a large number, and, which is passing strange, we are informed that many of the youths rose to wealth and eminence, founding pedigrees which ranked high in the state, among whom was the princely house of Vivaldi.[1] Those of noble rank naturally found a home with their own class, and so today even, many a Genoese, who rejoices in a proud title, may trace his ancestry back to some boy who, born by the Rhine, had been led by a mighty delusion to find a new home by the Mediterranean.

Those who desired to stay having secreted themselves, the rest of the band mournfully quitted the city where their hopes had been so cruelly shattered, amidst the jeers or the pity of the spectators, who lined the streets and the walls to see them depart, as they had done to see them arrive.

IV

To Rome

On Sunday, August 26th, the army which had so hopefully and proudly entered Genoa on the preceding day, issued with sad hearts from its gates.[2]

What is to be done now? they asked, as they gathered in the fields to deliberate. They could not return. No, better remain and die in sunny Italy, than perish in the mountains and the wilds which lay between them and home! The memory of the past two months was too vivid to allow any to desire to repeat their experiences.

But encouraging voices said: "Why yield to despondency? Are there no other cities which, more hospitable, will give us shelter and vessels to transport us to Palestine? Or, why think that Genoa was meant to be the place at which the way through

---

[1] Sicardi and Petrus Bizarus.
[2] Ogerius Panis, "Die Dominica sequente."

the sea was to be made? It may be elsewhere! Let us push on to the southward, until we find the passage which God has promised!" In this way they revived their drooping hopes and thought that theirs might yet be the happy destiny of kneeling on the sacred soil of Israel and returning from a successful Crusade.

Resolved to march by land, as far as they could, in the direction of Palestine, they turned their faces eastward, and soon the people of Genoa saw them pass out of sight over the hills. Their spirit was broken, however, and the disintegration, which had ceased for a while, was renewed. The people by the way induced many to remain, and compelled others. Many became daily more willing to secure homes in so fair a land and to exchange weary marching for repose.

And henceforth discipline seems to have been lost; they became an unregulated, headless band. Nicholas is not heard of again. It is not probable that his authority survived the disappointment at Genoa, where his many prophecies had been so signally falsified. He may have remained in that city or he may have departed from it with the army, but we can feel sure that he was no more the revered prophet that he had been.

Struggling on, the band of pilgrims journeyed through the mountain roads which lie to the eastward of Genoa. After many hardships, they reached Pisa, and gladly hailed its appearance, thinking it might be the hoped-for termination of their march. This city was then the rival of Genoa, and almost always its enemy in war. It was at this time in its prime. The streets, at present so deserted, which sadden the visitor by their silence, were full of busy life, and the Arno bore on its bosom countless vessels laden with the produce of all lands. On the quays and in the thoroughfares were seen as common things the bright and quaint costumes of the East, and the dark-hued children of warmer climes, who sojourned here for purposes of traffic; but that which astonished the stranger most of all

was meeting camels in the streets. Slaves of all races tugged
the oar of far wandering ships, and bore witness to the prowess
and the wealth of Pisa. There stood then, new and fresh, the
wonderful cathedral and baptistery, with the leaning campanile,
and, in the exquisite church of Santa Maria by the river, the
sailors prayed and gave votive offerings as they departed or as
they returned from sea.

Concerning their reception and stay in Pisa, we know but
little. That they were kindly received may be inferred in a
twofold way. In the first place, that Genoa had expelled them
would be a title to the hospitality of Pisa. And we are informed,
in the next place, that two shiploads of children sailed thence
to the Holy Land.[1] This fact is merely mentioned. To our
regret, we know not if they reached that destination. There
seems to be an indication, however, that they succeeded in
arriving at Ptolemais, then the only port in the hands of the
Christians. If they did, the Crusaders there must have thought
that there had been at home a cessation of authority and of
sense, to allow children to embark on so mad an enterprise,
and to add their hungry mouths to the population already scant
of food. Therefore if these children from Pisa reached the land
for which they hoped, it was only to be pent up in a beleaguered city, and to suffer and die of want and of disease.

Those who did not embark from Pisa left its walls and
sought to journey still farther southward, resolved to follow
the roads towards Palestine, as far as they would lead them.
They broke up into bands and groups and pursued different
routes. Florence and Arezzo saw them in their streets and wondered at their appearance. Perugia beheld them pass beneath
her rocky height, or else welcomed them in her walls, while
others took their way by Sienna. And, as they went through this
land of figs and of olives, the same story was repeated, of

[1] *Chron. Senoniense.*

enticement and of seizure, to which they submitted with few regrets.

At last a remnant of the original number who had left the place of gathering reached Rome, which was to be the limit of their journey. On some pleasant autumn day, they passed by Soracte, over the already ruin-strewed campagna, and greeted the great city where their faith centered.[1]

Strange must have been the contrast presented by Rome to those who came directly from the wealthy marts of Genoa and Pisa. Distracted by feuds, the city was impoverished, and squalid misery crouched among the crumbling remains of palaces and temples. This was the middle of that period of desolation which intervened between the ruin worked by the barbarians and the return of the present prosperity. Rome was, probably, at this time the most miserable city in Europe.

The children were brought before the Pope. Innocent was never known to feel or to yield to emotions of pity or of tenderness. His nature knew but little of kindness, and his conduct now showed his character. The children told their story of wandering, of suffering, of wrong, and of frustrated hopes. They rehearsed the account of their call by the Lord, and of the promises made to them, asking that he would assist them in prosecuting their journey, and give them encouragement and advice. Very naturally he praised their ardor and perseverance in so good a cause, but commanded them to desist from the further attempt to reach Palestine, showing the vanity of the enterprise. With a heartlessness born of his absorption in the cause of the Crusades, he said that nevertheless they could not be released from their vows; that they must, when they reached maturer years, redeem their promise to fight for the rescue of the Holy Sepulchre, whenever he should call upon them. He also sent word abroad to all who had returned or who had

[1] *Chron. Argenteum.*

found homes by the way that they would be likewise held to their assumption of the Cross, and that exceptions would only be made in favor of the aged who had joined in the movement, and of the very young, who could not have understood the language of the promise when they made it. In this way were the children bound to a repetition of their adventures and hardships. One writer justifies this edict of Innocent, comparing it to the fulfillment of Jephthah's vow.[1]

Here the journey of the army which left Cologne under Nicholas ended at last, and we close its story. The few who had reached Rome prepared to return homeward, their hopes all given up, and their dreams of triumph and of glory forever abandoned.

The few particulars which have been preserved concerning their return will be related when we reach the termination of the march of the other army, as the features of the homeward journey of both bands were similar.

We now turn again to those who had not left Cologne under the leadership of Nicholas.

[1] Herter, in his *Life of Innocent III.*

[CHAPTER V]

The Army with the Unknown Leader

Over the army which departed from Cologne under leadership other than that of Nicholas, there hangs, to our regret, great obscurity. Of its adventures but little detail has been preserved. Who its commander was, we do not know. He, who enjoyed the praises of thousands and reveled in the adulation of a host, surely thought that the part he played was destined to be forever memorable and that his name would be recalled when others of contemporary fame were forgotten. As he contrasted his task, which was to lead the Lord's children to a bloodless victory, with the exploits of the soldiers and nobles who were fighting for rival claimants of a crown, he doubtless imagined that, when the wars of Otho and of Frederick had been dropped by the Muse of History as trifling, she would linger long and fondly over the record of the rescue of the Holy City and the reinstatement of the Savior's worship among scenes consecrated by the story of his Incarnation. But his hopes were vain and his dreams of glory delusive. Less fortunate than his two fellow-leaders in the same Crusade, he has been forgotten, and there exists today, as far as can be ascertained, no clue to his name. It may yet be found in the unfrequented library of some old monastery, or in the dusty alcoves of some other repository of the learning and the piety of other days.

Nor do we know why the children at Cologne divided; why they did not unite under Nicholas. We are only told their route in general terms, and a few particulars of the issue of their journey.

They pursued a route which was longer; taking a circuitous course through Swabia, to the frontiers of what we now call Switzerland. In numbers they equaled those under Nicholas and were equally heterogeneous. There were many adults, male and female, old and young, wicked and pious. There was equal variety in the classes and ranks from whence recruits were won, and in all respects the assemblage was as motley and as ungovernable. It is possible that this variety produced such disorganization that, whoever may have led them at first, ere long all semblance of authority was lost, and the people only saw an undisciplined, and, as they thought, a headless throng. In this way we may account for the loss of the name of this rival of Nicholas.

On some unrecorded day—it may have been before or after the departure of that other misguided host whose journey we have described—this band passed across the Rhine and soon disappeared from the gaze of those who watched them from the river's bank. Why they chose this course we do not know; it may have been to gain new adherents, and to carry the excitement to districts which had not been aroused. The same circumstances attended their march as that of the others. They bore crosses and flags and sang songs and hymns to beguile the tedious hours. As they passed along, the laborers quitted their toil, the young ran away to follow them, and they left in their wake a series of childless homes. In their presence, the contesting bands of the Emperor and his insurgent subject ceased to fight. Towns and cities received them, in sympathy or in fear.

And they met also with the same vicissitudes. The depraved plied arts of infamy, and the thieves stole their money and their food. The journey wearied them, and want joined fatigue to breed and foster disease. The lawless nobles seized stragglers to carry them to their castles, which, now in such peaceful ruins, crown the hills and crags of central Germany. From hardship to hardship they persisted, losing heart at each step, until, having passed the lands watered by the Main and the Neckar, they reached the Danube. From there they marched on, until they stood by the Rhine again, probably near to where it issues from Lake Constance. Crossing this, they passed through Switzerland and reached the banks of Lake Lucerne. As they intended to cross the Alps by the pass of St. Gotthard, then next in importance to that of Mont Cenis, they had to sail the length of this beautiful sheet of water, for no path led around its perpendicular and uninhabitable shores.

Very, very suggestive is it to imagine them passing up this lake, and especially up the weirdly magnificent Bay of Uri, whose cliffs were then as silent as they are now. More silent they could not have been, for all the increase of population of modern days and the progress of science have resulted in no more disturbance than the plash of the little steamer's wheel, which wakes the lesser echoes of these mighty mountains only for a moment. Upon those fathomless blue waters we see them moving in many skiffs, their banners waving in the air, and their hearts thrilled by the grandeur of the scenery. What a sight it must have been! This lake had not yet the history which renders it so hallowed today. Grütli, where ninety-five years later the immortal three, Stauffacher, Fürst, and Melchthal were to meet and, in that moonlight conspiracy, to form the little confederacy of which Switzerland was born, was then an unnamed meadow, and flowers grew undisturbed upon the rock where now there stands Tell's Chapel in beauty which defies forgetfulness.

They reached the head of the lake and, disembarking, prepared to tread the path which led over the Alps to the sunny lands of the south. Thirty miles of weary climbing were to be achieved before the top was reached. There was no road. A wretched path wound from side to side of deep gorges and from peril to peril, often obliterated or swept away by the snows and torrents. Frequently the frail bridges, made in the spring, had been also washed away, and the children had to wade through the freezing waters which carried off, in their violence, more than one who could not resist the rushing, chilling stream. Those who have followed this route, even upon the present fine causeway, well remember the gloom of its defiles, the giddiness of its precipices, the awe-inspiring effect of the lofty mountains above, and the ceaseless roar of the cataracts below. Let such imagine the emotions of the little ones who trod this path seven hundred years ago! But, of all places, one appalls the traveler today more than any other. Between two perpendicular walls of rock rushes, in concentrated force, the foaming Reuss. Within this chasm there springs from side to side the Devil's Bridge. As we now cross the strong and noble arch which carries the road over the yawning abyss, we cannot fail to shudder at the precariousness of the ancient route, which was only superseded within the present century. The path then led for quite a distance along an uneven shelf that projected about a yard from the face of the perpendicular cliff, until directly in front of a cataract. From this ledge the bridge, hardly four feet wide, sprang to the opposite side, where the path was resumed, almost as dizzy as before. In fact so difficult was it to understand how an arch had been built here that the people attributed its origin to Satan. They said that, after many unsuccessful attempts had been made to construct a bridge and prevent the frequent loss of life, a man undertook the task, who came to the conclusion that no mortal could build one in that place. Then there appeared to him that person so active in records of the Middle Ages, the Devil. He said that he would complete the contract, if he were to have, as his pay, the soul of the first one that passed over the work. The bargain was gladly closed, and the next morning revealed a fine stone arch, spanning the conquered chasm. The happy man kept his agreement, but, with a pious regard for human welfare, sent over it first—his dog. The enraged architect seized a rock and threw it to ruin his work, but Providence diverted it, so that it fell, where it still lies, in the bed of the stream below.

Through scenes so wild did our children pass, and over other bridges almost as precarious. It needs not the record of the chronicler to tell us that many met death in these gloomy scenes of Uri. They died from hunger and fatigue, from disease and exposure. Avalanches and streams swept them away as they unwarily crossed their courses. Others, when the valleys were shrouded in mist, strayed from the path and wandered off into lateral gorges, where they lay down exhausted, on moors or in ravines, to sleep away their lives. The Alpine rose was beautiful, but it could give no sympathy. The springs sang cheerily, but they sounded as mockery. Worn out, bodily and mentally, hundreds, who in wanderings of mind saw vividly their once unvalued but now beloved homes, with children's grief and children's timidity, sobbed till they ceased to breathe. Over their remains no requiem was sung, except the voice of torrents; no weeping was heard but the sighing of the wind through the firs, which seemed responsive to their sighs; no monument was reared, except the wild flowers which, when spring came again, were nurtured by their dust; while the lofty mountain peaks, which kissed the sky and caught the clouds, pointed upward to their rest. We often hear or read of the sadness and interest of the graves of ocean, but not less secret or touching are the sepulchres on trackless mountain heights.

On the top of the pass there stood, as stands today, a monastery like that on Mont Cenis, where the traveler or pilgrim could rest or take refuge. We can imagine the astonishment of the good monks when they saw a vast procession of youths, ragged and weary, issuing from the gorges and commencing to file across the plain on which the hospice stood. They rubbed their eyes, but did not rub away the vision, for it was real, and

they soon learned, to their additional surprise, that this was the
Lord's army on the way to Jerusalem. The band tarried a while,
ate what food was provided; it may be they slept there, and
then proceeded to descend the pass. A day or two brought
them to the lovely plains of Lombardy, whose cultivation and
richness revived their spirits. But Italy was to be to them, as to
those led by Nicholas, no friendly land. During his long wars,
Barbarossa had repeatedly ravaged this region, and he had
excelled himself in the destruction of beautiful and ancient
Milan. These injuries were still fresh in the hearts of the people,
and we are expressly informed that they made these children
of the hated race feel that they had been unfortunate in their
choice of a route. Full of enmity, they made the young Crusaders pay for the excesses of their countrymen, so that their
journey was stained with tears and blood. Many were murdered; others were stolen to be carried away to misery, dishonor,
and slavery.

But they persevered, expecting, as the other band, to find a
pathway through the sea, when they had reached the end of
their journey by land. It was a long march along that road that
lay to the east of the Apennines. When they came to Ravenna,
or some other city, they were disappointed to find in each case
that it was not the place where the waters were to be divided
for them. At times, as in Umbria and by Ancona, they had
mountains to pass over, and as here or when near the shore
they saw the blue Adriatic, how welcome were the cool breezes,
how earnestly did they long to cross its waters! How inter-
minable must that journey have seemed! Of course they knew
nothing of geography, and as the names of places were told
them by the people whom they saw, they conveyed no idea
whether the goal they sought was far or near. They only knew
that, if they traveled long enough, they would reach the
extreme point of Italy, which was nearest to the Holy Land,
and there, surely, God would interfere to promote their farther

progress. In this hope they toiled on, by village and town, by frequent shrine and wayside cross; now in a cool valley, soon afterwards upon some fetid marsh; today under the shadow of the dark mountains, tomorrow on some waving campagna. Was there to be no respite to all this? Are we to see our comrades fall away and die, until none remain? Questions such as these were daily asked. At length they reached Apulia. Here new trials awaited them. They came now to traverse a stricken land, for it writhed under the tortures of famine caused by the drought of which we have spoken before. They had succeeded, by begging and gathering fruits along the way, in gaining a scanty supply of food, but now they were to be dependent upon the alms of a starving people. All the excesses of dearth were visible, and, instead of the usually luxurious crops of Italy's genial soil and climate, the Crusaders beheld fruitless trees, and parched fields whereon waved stunted stalks that bore no grain. So great was the want, so memorable the suffering that their report spread to distant Cremona, and its bishop, Sicardi, tells us, in strongest language, of the terrors of the season, adding that mothers in their hunger ate their children. It needs no long statement of chroniclers to portray the scenes witnessed as a band of unprovided children, emaciated and fatigued with marching, journeyed through this famishing region.

Causes above alluded to had tended to the diminution of their numbers, all the way from the Rhine to this point, and there now remained but a small fraction of the numerous company, who had entered upon their expedition so confident of easy march to sure success. But this remainder was again lessened by the hardships of Apulia, and each day saw many dying, returning, or straggling away, to be lost in a vain search for food.

A considerable number at length reached Brundusium, almost at the extremity of the Italian peninsula. This was in ancient days an important place and at this time was the principal port on that coast, having commerce with Eastern lands to which its situation adapted it.

Here then we find the children at last, after their long march over a route where all forms of difficulty had been encountered.

They who reached this point, although they had shown such endurance that they had borne up under every kind of temptation and trial, were now ready to confess that, if there was provided no sign of any intervention of God in their behalf, they would desist from further attempts. Would that we knew how many there were who entered the quaint and dirty streets of Brindisi, as it is now called, on that August or September day! We know their state. We know that their garments, so tattered, bore little evidence of having once been a uniform, and that they had not such bright ensigns, nor so many crosses as they had taken from Cologne. But as to number, we have no indication to guide us. All that can be said is that two or three thousand are as many as could be expected to remain, after such an incessant decimation.

Concerning their reception in Brindisi, we have some information. We learn that they were treated with extreme cruelty, and that they found its people even baser than those who lived to the northward. The girls were maltreated, seized, and decoyed away, and all the privileges of their character of pilgrims were despised. As the girls were thus treated, we can justly infer that the boys did not escape, but that they found it a city of sorrow. What its state must have been can easily be conceived, when we think upon the condition of Italy. In a few cities were centered all the light and all the civilization of the times, and in places so remote as Brindisi were to be found without alleviation the misery, the ignorance, and the irreligion of the dark ages. They who today visit it and find it worse than cities such as Capua or Terni, or those of lower Italy in general can form some idea of what it must have been in the thirteenth century.

But the bishop of this evil city, whose name has been forgotten, seems to have been a kind-hearted man. He is said to have understood the fraud of which the children were victims, and to have labored to undeceive them. He told them of the futility of their enterprise and of the sin of their disobedience, and then entreated them to return, instead of encountering the dangers that were still to be surmounted before the Holy Land would be reached.[1]

Most of them listened to advice so obviously wise, enforced by an experience so memorable as that of their journey. But many nevertheless wished to persevere, and these embarked in several ships, whose owners offered to convey them to the goal of their desires. They were deaf to all remonstrances and departed for the shores of the land in which they longed to rest.

They were never heard of again. They sailed away from the blue headlands of Cavallo, watched with strange interest by the people of Brindisi. And they sailed away into oblivion and silence, for where they died—whether in the hour of shipwreck on some lone rock in the sea, or in slavery in heathen lands, or yet in battle with the Saracen—shall not be known to mortals, until the day when "the earth and the sea shall give up their dead."

[1] Herter briefly gives these facts regarding Brindisi, from authorities I have not been able to find.

CHAPTER VI

The Return of the German Children

There are various hints and statements scattered among the chronicles, concerning the homeward wanderings of the German children, which may be briefly summed up. The reader may consider the relation of the experience of these little Crusaders monotonous, as a constant repetition of hardships and trials. It is natural to think how much greater would have been the interest of the narrative, if we knew more of the reception they met in the cities of Italy or Germany, if we had details of their adventures, and could associate definite spots with certain incidents of their pilgrimage. Episodes of romance must have been frequent, for we cannot imagine otherwise, when we think of hosts of children marching from place to place in an age so strange, passing by walls and towers which we now regard with veneration, and which we visit to recall the departed past. There must have been also many events of interest which attended the return of these youths, when they sought, in tears and regret, their homes again. As we look upon the route from Genoa, or Rome, from Brindisi, or Lombardy, we can find food for many fancies, in picturing their northward journey. But only a few particulars are preserved, and they are told us in general terms.

It has been seen how the children of both of the armies, whose march we have traced, dropped away from day to day, and how in this way the columns gradually diminished, until only a fraction of the original numbers reached the termination of the pilgrimage.

As was to be expected, when liberated from all restraint, they fell a prey to vice in the various cities of Italy, while in their condition of exhaustion and of want they were ready to listen to any temptations. The result was that every city and town through which they passed retained numbers of them, especially of the girls. Years afterwards travelers found them still there, sunken in vice and lost to purity. It is stated that for a long time they formed a large element in the depraved classes of the land. According to one chronicle, Brindisi has to bear the charge of being peculiarly fatal to virtue. It says:

> Illi de Brundusio virgines stuprantur.
> Et in arcum pessimum passim venumdantur.[1]

TRANSLATION

> The maidens were defiled in Brindisi
> And sold far and wide to the most evil money grubbers.

Many, however, remained from better motives, and to lead lives of industry in a land which was so enticing to those born in a region where neither nature nor art had done much for luxury and comfort. As it happened in Genoa, it was the case that in other cities numbers remained to mingle their blood with that of the dark Italians, and, in the pursuit of ease and wealth, to forget their dreams of fame and the associations of their childhood.

Yet most of them persisted in returning. There were to be seen frequent groups from both bands passing through the towns along the way. As they journeyed, they constantly came upon traces of their predecessors, and slept night after night by the scenes of former encampments and by nameless graves. The people who had seen them hurrying southward with some order and discipline now saw them returning in disorderly

[1] *Anon. Chron. Rhythmicum.*

companies, which were an easier prey than ever to the lawless. The land had been inhospitable before, but the few who may have been kind to them then had no care for them when foiled and disappointed.

And when they had crossed the Alps and stood on German soil where they had hoped for kindly treatment, they learned again that it was one thing to belong to a large and enthusiastic army which was seeking to rescue the Sepulchre, and another to be a defeated and worn-out penitent coming home. As one sympathizingly says, who may have seen some of them, "They who used to pass through countries in parties and troops and never without the song of encouragement now returned singly and in silence, barefooted and famished. They were a scoffing to all men." [1] He also adds that not only did the misery of their appearance contribute to render them subjects of scorn, and liable to reproach and cruelty, but their conduct was such, their morals so ruined by the experiences of the past, that they were repelled and despised by the same persons who once had regarded them as pious deliverers of the Holy Land. We can well believe that there were many of the groups who so conducted themselves that others succeeding them fared the worse. But even where there was no motive for retaliation, the treatment the children received from their countrymen was most cruel. Loading them with reproaches and taunts, they now turned away from their doors those to whom not long before they had not dared or wished to refuse food and shelter.

Consequently, their pathway through Germany to their homes was as trying as it had been in Italy, and they sickened and died, from exhaustion and starvation, in a land to which they had looked forward with fondness, and hope of reaching which had nerved them to cross again the terrible Alps. And when they had breathed out their weary lives, the barbarous

[1] *Chron. Argent.*

people would not bury their corpses, but in heartless inhumanity let them rot by the wayside.[1]

Day by day, there came straggling into Cologne, or the other cities from whence they had departed, groups of these victims of a sad delusion, their heads drooping in shame, their eyes red with tears, their clothing in rags. They bore not home their insignia, their banners, and their crosses. They had cast them away when they had learned the folly of their proud boasts, and the vanity of this display. They sought again the lowly hut and the baronial castle, where, at last, they rested, home again! Alas! how they had paid for their willfulness! They were asked where they had been, and we are told that they replied that they "did not know!" They only knew of days of varied vicissitude. They knew not, in their ignorance, what had been their route, what lands they had traversed, or what cities they had seen. They had journeyed until they could journey no longer, and then they had turned homeward. What a confused and wild story did they tell, of strange languages and costumes, of curious edifices and wonderful fruits! How many days elapsed before they had answered all the questions which their friends, in mingled wonder and pity, asked of those who had survived! And those who had not survived! How eagerly were they inquired after! How anxiously did parents greet each band to ascertain whether their own dear ones had yet come! How many hearts were kept in suspense for days and weeks, while the companies continued to arrive, until they found the children they cared for, or else learned their fate, that they had died in the forest or on the mountain, on the plain or in the valley, or had remained in some distant Italian city, to return no more! There was many a Rachel by the Rhine and the Moselle, by the Meuse and the Lippe, who wept long years for children dead or forever separated from them.

[1] *Gesta Trevirorum.*

The winter had passed, and the following spring had come and gone, before the last company came struggling back. Soon the excitement died away, and, in the confusion and ravages of war, the sorrows and adventures of the little Crusaders were forgotten by the same people who had rushed to see them depart, and who had wondered at the issue of their enterprise.

Yet, for many years were they remembered by those who had been partakers in the movement, or by those who had lost a beloved one in its whirl. Long afterwards did peasant, noble, shepherd, and merchant gather with ever new interest to hear the old story, and many a child became a father, to tell to little ones around him the tear-awakening tale of what he had seen and suffered, when in childhood he set out in credulous enthusiasm "to seek the Cross beyond the sea."

Thus have we, imperfectly enough, attempted to tell the story of the Crusade of the German children, which arose from the preaching of Nicholas at the shrine of the Kings.

Tersely does an old epigram sum up the whole matter: [1]

> Ad mare stultorum
> Tendebat iter puerorum.

[1] Quoted by Herter from an unknown source:

> To the sea of fools
> Led the path of the children.

CHAPTER VII

The Journey of the French Children

I

The Gathering at Vendôme

We left Stephen preaching at St. Denys and his youthful lieutenants gathering children from various parts of France. This
continued long after the German army had started and the
latter was well on its way to Italy before the French little ones
were ready to begin their journey. The probable reason for this
was that the movement was spread over a greater extent of
country, and therefore the collecting of an army required a
longer time.

Stephen indicated Vendôme as the place of assembling and
of united departure for Palestine.[1] This city had the advantages
of being central and near to his home. It was a town of importance and from it there diverged roads in all directions.

During the latter part of June the various bands continued
to arrive in this city, all led by a common enthusiasm and full
of common hopes. Very stirring must have been the streets as
daily some new company came with its young prophet and loud
were the noises of their greetings. We can imagine how it must
have seemed to look across the plains and see some group coming over the distant hills, or defiling across the country, their
flags and oriflammes waving high in air and crosses rising
higher yet. As they approach, their songs are heard, first faint
in the distance and then clearer and louder until the words are
distinct, and the dialect discloses the region whence they come.

---

[1] All the chronicles agree in this.

For they arrived from each province, with their different languages and costumes and peculiarities—some speaking the soft accents of the south, others the harsher dialects of Brittany or Normandy; some the langue d'Oc, others the langue d'Oil. Very great were the consequent confusion and the variety in the composition of the assembling army, which was to march to bloodless glory under Stephen. The largest band which came to the gathering was that from Paris. Of this company a chronicler says that there were collected in that city "fifteen thousand, of whom none were more than twelve years of age," [1] a statement which we may take with caution, but at the same time it shows, as do many others similar, relating to the event, how very young the children really were and how great their numbers. The cause of so many being recruited in Paris was its proximity to St. Denys, as well as its being the capital and principal city of the realm. The march of this body to Vendôme must have been peculiarly imposing, and their arrival the great excitement of exciting days. The crowds gathering here were therefore still more motley than those at Cologne, as regards diversity of customs and of dialects. There were the same kinds of hangers-on mingled with the boys. The number of depraved men and women was as great, and they came from every quarter of France to profit by so unique an opportunity. There were also many girls, some of whom, afraid of detection, assumed male attire. But, although there was a large proportion of these men and women and girls attracted by motives of a base or of a pious nature, it is nevertheless true that their number was relatively smaller than it was in the German armies, and therefore this movement is more interesting, from being more exclusively one of boys.

Yet, however varied their languages and different their dresses and customs, they all were one in their feelings and

[1] Roger de Wendover.

understood one another in the sympathy of a common, beloved cause. Repeating the promises of their leaders, for it was with them as with the Germans in this respect, they all said that they were not to wait, as their predecessors in the holy war had done, for vessels to carry them to Palestine, and in them to find, as had so many brave men, a grave in the wide Mediterranean. "Between waters, which are to be to us as a wall on the right hand and on the left, are we to cross the untrodden bed of the sea, and, with dry feet will we stand on the distant beach by the walls of Acre or of Tripoli. We bear no weapons and we wear no armor! The pathway of other Crusaders may be marked by the stain of blood and the glitter of steel, and martial music may have timed their many steps, but our pilgrim's robes are our armor, our Crosses are our swords, and our hymns shall time our march!"

We are not told whether they assumed any general uniform, but the analogy of all other Crusades and scattered hints would seem to indicate that all who could procure it wore a prescribed dress. They all wore the Cross at least. This was made of woolen cloth, and sewed on the right shoulder of the coat. To place it there was a duty reserved to the prophets alone, as it was the formal act of enlistment. The little fellows were as proud of them as the young officer of his epaulettes and were beside themselves with joy at being thus enrolled among the Crusaders and in a company which contained so many famous names, the recollection of whose deeds fired every heart with a desire to equal their achievements.

As their numbers were too great to be contained within the city, they encamped without its walls, each band by itself and keeping its identity until merged into the common mass at departure. Day by day they waited, as recruits continued to arrive. The monks and priests who had joined them, either in piety to guide them or as pilgrims themselves, aided the young leaders in maintaining the spirit of enthusiasm and in promoting unity and peace. The discouraged were cheered, the homesick consoled, and the depraved, as far as possible, expelled.

At last, the latest band had come, and Stephen announced that they were ready to start. The number then assembled around Vendôme was about thirty thousand,[1] as all the estimates warrant us in concluding. What an uprising of homes this was! How sad a scene to the thoughtful who foresaw the certain fate of that vast multitude! It was to melt away that same autumn, as the snows of winter, and when a year had rolled around and brought another summer, but few of them were to be at home again. Many would fill graves among strangers or in the deep sea! For the summer was well advanced, and it was at least the end of July when in the camps was heard the bustle of departure. We will now follow these thirty thousand children seeking, in the heat of August, the port of Marseilles, where they were to find that wonderful pathway through the sea.

II

The Journey to Marseilles

The fields around Vendôme had never seen before and never shall see again a sight like that which on that day was witnessed, when the army of children formed its ranks, to commence its chimerical pilgrimage. Pleading relatives and weeping friends were mingled with admirers, and entreaties to repent and remain were met and counteracted by applause and encouragement. The latter form of advice accorded with their wishes, and the deluded youths answered the arguments of dissuasion with the wild and baseless assertions which they had heard from those who urged them onward. It was too late to reason now. To withdraw was impossible, if desired. They could not encounter the ridicule of abandoning their comrades in this the hour of hope. After religious exercises, wherein

---

[1] Albericus; Vincent de Beauvais; *Chron. Laon;* Jean d'Ypres.

the blessing of God was invoked, the oriflammes and Crosses were raised in gladness, and with visions of pleasant wanderings to triumphant rest, these thousands of children commenced their journey.

Their route was to lie by Blois, where the ancient road crossed the Loire, in a southeasterly direction to the Rhône, and thence southward to Marseilles. Far different was this journey from that of the Germans, for there were no Alpine heights or Alpine torrents, and the country was not so little civilized and unpeopled as that which intervened between Cologne and Italy. The result of this difference was that the hardships of the band whom we are now to follow were very much less than those which we have described.

Childlike was their ardor as they began to tread the way to Palestine. They looked on the red Crosses on their shoulders in order to acquire that resolution in the holy cause which would enable them to exclude regrets for home and fear of fatigue. Determined to act as faithful soldiers in the army of God, they set their feet down at each step with manly firmness. There was a much better spirit among those composing this army than among those who departed from Cologne, owing to the presence of fewer depraved adults and youths. There were also very many ecclesiastics, and their presence was some restraint upon the tendencies to vice and dissension, while they also could encourage and advise the desponding.

They have departed from Vendôme, and as evening closes around the landscape, the people of that old city have seen disappear the last straggler of that army of children led by a child. Let us now turn to this leader, of whom little has been heard since he preached at St. Denys. Fortunately, the chroniclers have preserved to us some particulars concerning the deportment of this commander of Lilliputian Crusaders.

As would be expected, the applause and homage which Stephen received had turned his head, as has so often been the case with older persons. Elevated in a few weeks, from being an obscure shepherd boy in Cloyes for whom none cared, and accustomed to regard the nobles who despised his condition as unattainably above him to a station where he received the admiration of thousands, was regarded as a saint, and received adulatory obedience, he would have been more than human if he had not learned to be vain, to indulge in display, and to exact extreme reverence. Accordingly we find that, as he led his army from Vendôme, he assumed a pretense of pomp and presented a marked contrast with the appearance of those whom he commanded. He could not walk. That was too humble for such a leader. The Lord's own general and prophet must assume the style which became his rank. He therefore rode in a chariot, as splendid as could be procured, which was covered with rare carpets of brilliant colors. Over his head to protect him from the heat of the sun was a canopy, whence there hung in folds rich draperies of every hue. Around this chariot to guard him and carry out his commands as well as to add to the impressiveness of his station, there rode a band of chosen youths of noble birth, on chargers, dressed in splendid accoutrements, and armed with lances and spears.[1] They vied with each other in zeal in his behalf and gladly obeyed him whom once they would have spurned.

All this assumption of display does not seem to have shaken the confidence of his followers. It appears, on the contrary, to have increased it, upon principles which we can easily understand. Too young to see the inconsistency of his conduct, they listened to his words as those of God and regarded his desires as law. In order to maintain the spirit of the host, which fatigue would tend to lessen, he wisely addressed them often. When they departed in the morning from their resting place, or when they halted at noon or encamped at evening and also during

[1] Roger de Wendover, *inter al.*

the march, he spoke encouraging words from his chariot. It is said that on such occasions they thronged around him so tumultuously that it frequently required the strenuous efforts of his guards to protect him from the consequences of their eager homage, and that as they thus pushed and struggled in endeavors to approach the prophet boy, accidents occurred, many of those who were small and weak being crushed to death.

But such incidents made merely transient impressions on this thoughtless crowd. They forgot them all when some event awakened anew their enthusiasm. To such an extent was their regard for Stephen carried that it amounted to investing him with all the attributes of sanctity. They vied in efforts to procure from his person or his chariot some little fragment, which was kept as a relic and valued as a charm. They who had succeeded in securing a thread of his raiment, or a piece of the trappings of the car or even of the accoutrements of the horses, showed them with exultation to the others, while they who had a single hair of his head were regarded as possessors of a priceless treasure.

As regards the moral character of Stephen, one chronicler says: "He was a child in years but accomplished in vice." [1] But he wrote long after the event, and in his whole narrative is the conviction that Stephen had originated and carried out the deception and visits on this child's head all the disasters and sorrows which resulted. Of course, if he had been a willful deceiver and had acted a conscious fraud so cruelly and with so many lies, he would have been remarkably mature in depravity as well as in intellect. But if, as we have seen, it was the case that he was himself the subject of deception by a priest, then the above accusation, founded on the supposition of his originating the movement and fabricating the story of

[1] Roger de Wendover.

his call falls to the ground. And while, nevertheless, there may have been reasons for the assertion, still, other considerations render it difficult to believe that he was notoriously vicious. We can hardly think that the priest who sought him out would have chosen him as the instrument of arousing the country if he had won such a reputation; the very object in view would have been frustrated at once, if those who knew him could tell his dupes that such was his character. It is natural to suppose that he had something winning about him to gain so many adherents of all ages and classes, and that he was not known to be immoral, or else he would scarcely have received veneration as a saint. The very success of his preaching therefore leads us to believe that he was not known to be particularly bad. On the other hand, if we believe that he was duped and thought himself entrusted by Christ with the duty of proclaiming and conducting the Crusade, we would be led to suppose that he was piously disposed and felt what he uttered when he depicted the misery of the Christians in the Holy Land, and the ignominious state of the Sepulchre of the Savior. Nothing that we know concerning his conduct is inconsistent with childish piety. The state which he assumed does not contradict such a supposition, for it would have required the years and spirit of a Peter or of a Bernard to have been unaffected by flattery and luxury, after having been accustomed to the lot of the poor and to the scorn and abuse which that class received from the nobles.

We see in him, then, a child of twelve years of age, who was carried away with the belief that he was God's chosen leader to rescue Palestine and whose unreasoning mind was inflated by constant respect and adulation of a host. He was evidently precocious and possessed of no slight abilities, however much of the direction and control of the vast army which he led may be attributed to older persons with whom he consulted. For although no reference is made to such counselors, it is wild to suppose that there were none, but that he actually chose the route and regulated the march.

So they trudge wearily along, this host of deluded children, led by their child prophet, reclining at ease in his luxurious chariot. Their little limbs were not used to more than short journeys to and from the pastures where they had fed their flocks, and they soon learned that, although glory and honor were at the end of the pilgrimage, fatigue and suffering intervened. The girls and the children of gentle birth were especially unfitted to endure such a march, and when the first day ended, there were many blistered feet and tearful eyes.

As has been said, their pathway was marked by much fewer hardships than those of the German armies, inasmuch as the country was more peopled, as well as because the distance to be traversed was much shorter. They did not have to sleep on rocky heights or on freezing moors; they always found fields to rest in, and as they passed through no strange land, they received the sympathy of countrymen instead of the hostility of aliens. Consequently, as we shall see, their numbers were comparatively little affected by desertion and death. But yet it was not a path of roses; their journey was not unalloyed with trials.

Of course a frequent source of trouble was scarcity of food. There was no regular provision for its supply, and soon they were reduced to what they could beg. We are told that this was readily given, and even that money was furnished in many cases by the people who sympathized with them. But there were some districts which were uninhabited, and here they suffered from hunger and disease.

A great deal of misery was caused by the great heat of this summer, which, as we have seen, was of unusual intensity.[1]

---

[1] Lambert of Liège.

This caused the great drought of which we spoke when following the fortunes of the other armies, and here, as there, it was said to be the evident intervention of God to dry up the sea.

It was terrible to walk from day to day under a broiling sun, through fields that were parched and burned, where the brooks were dry, and the moss on the stones was dead, where morning brought no freshness, and evening no dew. This prostrated numbers of the children, and their corpses lay scattered along the road for many a mile.

These hardships and the influence of the unworthy characters soon resulted in more or less complete loss of discipline and of authority. Want produced dissensions and developed selfishness, each one being on the alert to outwit the others in the search for food and in endeavors to keep it concealed. They then straggled on, becoming more and more a loose, congregated horde, until at last Stephen's authority was entirely disregarded, and it was a race for the sea. Their spirits had been for a while kept up by the impulse of the original excitement; then they had sung their songs and told tales of adventure, and the leaders had artfully tried to make them forget fatigue in anticipation of the coming glory. For they had their songs as had the children of Germany, but they are all lost to us. With these they passed away many a monotonous hour, proclaiming their determination to rescue and restore to its honor the Sepulchre of Christ. Constantly renewed promises and imaginary descriptions of rest to be won were also effective in counteracting the desire to return, which their trials engendered, and kept together those who still persevered. Stephen was always wont to reply, and his lieutenants also, in answer to inquiries as to when the weary march would be over, that the end was near at hand, and that a few more days or hours would bring them to the sea. Their ignorance of geography rendered them unable to detect the falsehoods thus told them, and they were therefore repeatedly led to hope for the morrow, only to be grievously disappointed when that morrow came. Their innocence and confiding credulity are vividly represented by the statement of an historian,[1] who says that, as they thought of nothing but Jerusalem, and day by day were told that their toils would soon be over, when they came in sight of a castle or a walled town, some of them would ask, forgetful of the sea which intervened, "Is that Jerusalem?" Poor little pilgrims! How often have children of a larger growth, as they labored and toiled, fancied that they beheld in some prospect before them the Jerusalem they sought! And it reminds us also that possibly there was often heard among them that appeal which heralds in other crusading armies were wont to make to the weakhearted and weary, who were aroused to new effort when they heard it: "This is not Jerusalem!"

They passed through central France, crossing the Rhône, as was most usual, at Lyons, and then entered the kingdom of Burgundy or Arelate. The crusading spirit was peculiarly strong here, and the children received sympathy and aid. But nevertheless it was still a fatiguing march until they reached Provence, which seemed as a new world to them. This was the garden of all Europe. Among fields of unequaled luxuriance there stood moss-covered ruins of ancient days, which, by their frequency and elegance, showed how the Romans had prized the region and loved to embellish it.

Past broken aqueducts and roofless temples, they wandered in a beautiful country and began to forget the trials of a route through uninhabited districts and uncultivated wilds. Their spirits revived, and their hopes again were raised. Finally they reached the last range of hills they had to climb, when there burst upon them a view which awakened in them emotions of astonishment and delight. Before them was the cool, blue sea. The crisp waves broke on its bosom, and clouds chased each

[1] Choiseul d'Aillecourt.

other across its vast horizon, while beautiful islands dotted its surface here and there along the coast. Below them upon the shore was Marseilles, which, though not forming so enchanting a vision as Genoa, yet astonished these young pilgrims, who had never seen such a sight before. They hurried down to its walls. Songs of loud accord announced their coming to the people of the city, and they went out to meet this most curious of all the many curious armies that had come thither in order to embark on the historic Mediterranean.

III
Marseilles and the Good Merchants

After a long period of obscurity, Marseilles had at this time become again, as it had been centuries before, one of the chief cities on the shore of the Mediterranean. Since the days when it was able to resist so long the arms of Caesar, in upholding the interests of Pompey, there had intervened an era of poverty and of feebleness. It had been a part of the kingdom of Provence until A.D. 930, when the latter became united to Burgundy Transjurane. In A.D. 1032, this kingdom was inherited by the Emperor Conrad. But, as it was a remote dependency of the empire, the imperial rule rested lightly upon it; so lightly, indeed, that it was practically independent, under its own feudal counts, acting as a sovereign state, and making treaties with other powers. At the time of the event we are describing, it was still thus situated, but was on the verge of a revolution, for in 1214 the citizens expelled the Count, and, tempted and excited by the examples of sister cities, formed a republic which flourished until 1251, when the Count of Provence annexed the aspiring state to his own dominions. The chief cause of the recovery of the importance and influence of Marseilles was the Crusades. Its harbor being so secure, for a Mediterranean port, it was a great point for shipping men and supplies in the prosecution of the wars in the Orient. It was thence that Richard I departed in great state, and later still Louis IX was furnished by the town with all the ships which his vain enterprise required. During the preceding centuries, the classic cities of Nîmes, Narbonne, and Montpellier had risen to be the chief places of France, and, nestled amid their luxuriant fields and groves, they had become synonymous with splendor and wealth. But with the revival of commerce, Marseilles was destined to resume her precedence of these less ancient rivals, and already in 1212 her people anticipated even surpassing more favored Genoa or Pisa. Stately edifices were being erected by her ambitious citizens, and in the shipyards they were constructing those mighty vessels which were regarded as able to conquer the seas.

Such then was Marseilles when our young Crusaders reached it. The distance they had traveled was about three hundred miles, and the time nearly a month. It was therefore towards the middle of August when they arrived at their destination. Although they started later than the German children, they reached the sea at an earlier day, as their journey was so much shorter; and, when they were resting from their fatigues, the followers of Nicholas and of the other leader were yet suffering in the Alps or in Italy.

Many children had left the army on the way, and many more had succumbed to fatigue or had been captured. Yet the diminution of their numbers was not to be compared with that experienced by the German armies. One authority says that the number was almost as great as when they left Vendôme and that many new adherents had joined the throng to take the places of those who deserted or fell by the wayside. Therefore it was not a worn-out and tattered band, counting but a fraction of its original size, which reached Marseilles, as had been that one which greeted Genoa so gladly; but we see approaching the imposing number of at least twenty thousand children, who, though they had not reached Jerusalem as soon as they had hoped, still had their faith in their undertaking restored by arrival at the seashore.

Halting, then, by the walls, they asked for shelter in the city. As at Genoa, it was stated that temporary rest was all they needed; that, as God had promised to open for them a way through the sea, they would ask no vessels, require no prolonged hospitality, but that perhaps on the morrow they would depart. Congratulated should be the people of that city which was selected as the point of departure of those who, as the Lord's soldiers, were to pass in security, as Israel had done, through the waves which had ever been the terror of powerless mariners. Whether the Massilians appreciated the honor or not is another question. Having lived for some time by the seaside and not being credulous victims of a delusion, we may believe that they expected to have to make provision for some other mode of reaching Palestine and did not rely much upon the prospect of having their city placed in history by the side of Pi-hahiroth and Gilgal, as the scene of a miraculous control of the waters. On the contrary, many of the citizens were doubtless rejoiced at the chance of profiting by such an influx of pilgrims. The authorities may well have hesitated at admitting so formidable a host into the city, which did not even have the restraining influences of discipline, as was the case with older Crusaders. But there was a strong sympathy with the cause, and especially in view of the fact that the pilgrims were countrymen did they hesitate to refuse to shelter them; while, on the other hand, there was no political reason to awaken distrust or fear, and the city had too often provided for larger armies to be exhausted by one like this. Accordingly, permission to tarry was granted, and among the throngs of wondering people, the children, with their leaders, their priests, and their adult companions, entered the venerable gates. Their hymns were now sung with new earnestness, born of the encouragement of reaching so advanced a stage in their journey. Prouder than ever, they declared to the astonished beholders that they were to render brilliant with associations of victory, fields now for ages synonymous with defeat. The people, who had seen the hosts of Richard in their manly strength and with their splendid accoutrements enter the same gates with like high hopes twenty-two years before, may well have wondered at the simplicity of these youthful warriors. Some pitied them, as they thought of the rich harvest death was to reap where he had already reaped so many, and prayed they might be spared the sad fate which thousands had met who sought that land, the footsteps on the road to which, like those before the cave of the fabled monster, all pointed but in one direction. Others eagerly believed the story of divine interposition to raise this army and piously hoped that at last the object of so many toils and of so many prayers was to be attained.

The children dispersed and sought lodging where it was to be had. The youths of noble birth found rest with those of their kindred or of their rank. Others were received into inns and convents and monasteries. Others still, unable to find room, slept in those bed-chambers of the poor in every age—the streets.

That night, as they saw the darkness creep over the earth, they went to sleep, full of hope that in the morning the constantly repeated promise of Stephen would be realized, and that their mission would be confirmed, as well as doubters refuted, by the spectacle of a way through the deep waters.

The night passed away. Morning dawned, but its light showed a still unsevered expanse, presenting no path for the pilgrim's foot. The waves rolled and curled and broke as unrestrainedly as ever, and told as plainly of unbridled power. Great then was the perplexity of the children, but nevertheless they still hoped that another day might be more propitious. And they waited for that day, and for still another and another. But during this delay their numbers diminished rapidly.

The deception of the leaders became apparent, and the promises which had solaced them in weary marches, and kept up their courage, being so repeatedly falsified, they began to yield to despair and disgust. The army melted away, some departing each morning, when the pathway in the sea was again found unopened. However, there were still many who would not yield, but cherished the hope of reaching the Holy Land, and would wait longer for the appointed passage thither. They looked wistfully at the vessels in the harbor, and wished that if their promised pathway were not to be granted, they might seek their destination on these. But their poverty precluded the possibility of that, and as day by day they stood sadly watching the sea and yet found no realization of their hopes, even the most hopeful commenced to resign themselves to the belief that they had seen the end of a Crusade so triumphantly and so proudly begun. Throughout the ranks spread the determination to return, and in silent or in recriminating sorrow all prepared for a disgraceful retracing of their steps. They cursed the deceivers who had led them thus astray and reproached themselves as they thought of the taunts to be encountered on the return, which they dreaded more than they prized the joy of being at home again.

When in this sad plight, there came unexpected relief, and their discouragement was changed to exultation by an event which they considered a fulfillment of their hopes.

There were in Marseilles two merchants who drove a lucrative trade with other lands, and who, from their wealth, were clearly prominent men on the primitive "Change" of those days. Their names, in the French form, have not been preserved; the chroniclers tell them to us in Latin, and they figure in history under the euphonious appellations of Hugo Ferreus and William Porcus. Undoubtedly the wits of the city had enjoyed many a joke upon them, but the conduct of the men who bore them was now to show these wits that a man's character is not to be determined by his name. For as they heard the complaints and witnessed the heartrending disappointment of the little Crusaders, they were deeply moved. They saw them go down by the shore and in childish eagerness scan the horizon to find if there were no way to pass over the sea. The tears and cries of these weary, deluded ones, which awakened so much sympathy in all hearts, at last prompted these merchants to interfere and aid in the prosecution of a holy work apparently about to be frustrated. Accordingly, to the wonder and delight of all, they voluntarily offered to provide vessels to convey to Palestine as many as still desired to continue the pilgrimage. In their pious sympathy and interest in the defiled Sepulchre, they would ask of Christ's soldiers no money for their passage. They wished to do the deed, said they, *causa Dei, absque pretio,* "for the cause of God, and without price." All the reward they desired was the consciousness of duty done, the prayers of the child-warriors of God, and the honor of aiding in the final and successful effort to rescue sacred places from unholy rulers. What better gain could they ask than the fame of being the great benefactors of those who were to place the Cross above the insulting Crescent?

Great was the rejoicing now! Stephen and his lieutenant prophets triumphantly proclaimed that their predictions were verified and taunted the lack of faith of the discouraged. "This," said they, "was the vindication of their prophetic character! This was the way through the sea which God had meant! Was it not a miracle? Was it not a fulfillment of his promise that they would find a path across the deep waters? All other Crusaders and all other pilgrims had been obliged to pay heavily for their conveyance to Palestine, yet it was to cost them nothing! What better evidence of God's sanction and aid could there be than this, that an obstacle, so insurmountable to others, had been removed for them?"

There were those, however, who did not yield to the newly

awakened enthusiasm. They had learned to dread the sea, from the many adventures of peril of which they had heard during the previous Crusades, and while they would have readily marched upon its bed, they feared to sail upon its surface. They gazed on its unbounded expanse, and its vastness awed them. They had seen vessels come into port, rolling from side to side and dashing the spray from their bows, and there was no charm for them in the idea of trusting themselves to its treacherous power. But there were many others who were willing to brave all this if they could only reach Jerusalem. The Lord, who sent the vessels, could guide and guard them. Their vows, their Crosses on their breasts, their promises, and their pride made these resolve to persevere and seek the sacred shores.

Accordingly, all who were willing to embrace the offer of the merchants reported themselves, and it was ascertained that seven vessels would be required for their transportation. From this we may, in connection with other data, conjecture how many they numbered. We find, for instance, that in the expedition of Saint Louis there were seven hundred on each ship, and we cannot be far wrong in supposing that the merchants would at least allot as many children to each of their vessels. There would be then, we conclude, nearly five thousand to be provided for by these kindhearted men. So we are reasonably led to believe that this, or one-sixth of the original host which left Vendôme, was the number of those who expressed their readiness after so many discouragements to embark upon the sea. Among them, as we shall see in the sequel, were many adults, priests, and other ecclesiastics, who really may never have expected to cross the Mediterranean in any other way, and to whom the perils of navigation were not unanticipated.

We now see the enterprising and benevolent merchants preparing their vessels for the departure of the earnest little Crusaders, who would not return unless they came as deliverers of the Sepulchre. The inhabitants of Marseilles were proud of their townsmen's liberality and of the fact that they possessed citizens able to afford so munificent a benefaction. Their praises were on every lip, and the people lent their lively interest in behalf of an enterprise which, once so apparently vain, now promised such success.

IV

The Embarkation

When we look through the chronicles of the days to which our story carries us, we are entertained by the many and quaint names by which the different kinds of vessels were distinguished. We read enthusiastic accounts of the grace, the elegance, and speed of their galleys, designed both to convey passengers and for purposes of war. Those of similar style but of smaller size were galleons, employed for light work, and for skirmishing. We then read of busses, or buzas, which were used chiefly for commerce and were consequently more clumsy, while the simplehearted old writers who in their cloistered homes had never seen such things, descant with wonder on the gigantic dromons, the largest barks that ploughed the sea, and whose mention suggested wealth that astonished the landsman and made the pirate sleepless. And some, with a superabundance of nautical lore, probably to show that knowledge, dilate upon the speed and the size, the mishaps and adventures of gulafres, cats, and other undescribed triumphs of human ingenuity. The language which is employed by Richard of Devizes, or Geoffrey de Vinsauf, or Joinville concerning the ships which bore Richard I and Louis IX across the waters, would lead us to picture these heroes as sailing on vessels like those which astonish us today. In the light of modern achievements in the construction of vessels, it sounds rather amusing to hear the qualifications "gigantic," "towering," "mighty" applied to boats of two hundred, or, at the most, three hundred tons. It was not until the emergencies of later ages and the development of the

arts and sciences that larger hulks were built. At this time a
great change was taking place in navigation. The use of oars
was being discarded, and vessels were made to be propelled
entirely by the wind. Some of the dromons are said, wonderful
to relate, to have had three masts! There were no graceful
stems which divided the waters like knives. The waves were
pushed aside by broad bows, which presented tempting ex-
panses for those waves to retaliate by buffetings. Instead of
delicate sterns, whose graceful curves would scarcely cause a
perceptible wake, angular, clumsy surfaces sustained a lofty
and perilous poop, and the entire form of the structure was
eminently adapted to unlimited rolling and pitching, evidence
of which is furnished by the constantly narrated miseries of
voyagers.

As regards the vessels provided by the merchants, the rate
at which they traveled, as we shall subsequently see, shows that
they were propelled by sails. But whether the seven ships, which
in the port of Marseilles awaited their precious burdens, were
gulafres, or galleys, or cats, or dromons, or buzas, to those who
were accustomed only to the barks which floated on the Seine
or the Loire or the Rhône, they seemed immense monsters,
and reassured the hearts of the little ones by their evident
ability to conquer the deep and brave in safety perils of wind,
of water, or of reef.

At last the preparations were all completed, and the day
dawned when the young heroes were to leave their native
shores and seek those whither had gone so many other hosts,
as full of hope, to find only misery and death.[1] The sun, as it
gilded with its first rays the hills around the city, called from
sleepless couches the excited and anxious children, who today
were to become real Crusaders, and, like other brave heroes,
to sail out upon the sea. They passed the necessary time in

[1] For ceremonies attending embarkation, see Joinville and other crusading
chroniclers.

religious preparation, thronging the churches to receive blessings and absolutions, and then sought the water's edge to await embarkation. Very striking must the spectacle have been, when in that landlocked bay the vessels were waiting with flags flying, and when along the shore the citizens, attracted by the interest and novelty of the event, crowded to behold the scene. The gaudy colors of the banners and of the dresses of the groups upon the beach blended with the golden tints in which the fronts of the quaint old houses were bathed, and with the blue water and the azure sky made a picture on which imagination fondly dwells.

It was natural for the people to contrast the embarkation of these Crusaders with the last departure of an army from that port, bound on a similar enterprise. It had occurred twenty-two years before, when, in 1190, Richard I of England had sailed from thence to Messina, where he was to meet Philip of France, from which place they proceeded together to Palestine. That had been a notable sight. There were "one hundred and fourteen vessels of great magnitude," and at the masthead of each flew the ensign of England's king. The historian, sober Richard of Devizes, a credulous and honest old soul, tells us that "there was on each ship double of whatever a ship could want, except the mast and the ship's boat; a fleet wonderful for its numbers, complement, and the splendor of its array, and the like of which none was ever seen, fitted out with such labor, and so numerous." But now the Massilians saw a few thousand children about to embark on seven vessels, with no king or prince to lead them, no bright armor or glittering lances, no flag that told of victories, but, nevertheless, as confident and as hopeful as the warriors who had preceded them on the pathway to Palestine. How many were there in that crowd of observers who foresaw the certain issue of this enterprise! They had seen the army of Richard depart but to perish, and they judged well that where those heroes had fallen, these children would not succeed. It may be that some were present who had been beyond the seas and knew by bitter experience the perils of the deep and the character of the Moslem enemy, and they shuddered at the vision which was conjured up as they thought of so many children falling into the power of those heathen.

The embarkation proceeded. Entering into skiffs, the youths were borne to the vessels amidst the sad farewells of friends who loved them, and of companions who feared to continue the undertaking, which they had vowed to complete ere they knew its dangers, as well as amidst the cheers of the enthusiastic and of the sympathizing. Steeling their little hearts against discouragement and dread, they left the shore in companies, until the last one had stepped from the soil of France. When the ships were full, the ports through which they had entered were closed, and they within, as well as those on the beach, were reminded that there was now no withdrawing, no retreat.

The ceremonies attending setting sail were solemn, because in those times it was a serious thing to commence a voyage over the sea, and the nature of the enterprise made religious rites appropriate and customary.

The captains examined all parts of the ships to make certain that they were in proper order for such a dangerous voyage. As one says, "The ports were stopped up as close as a large tun of wine." The sailors were stationed at their respective posts; the anchor chains were loosened, ready to release the vessels in a moment, and the sheets held in hand. All being thus prepared, silence ensued for a brief space of time. Then upon the elevated "castle" or stern of each ship, the assembled priests in sweet accord commenced to chant that dear old hymn, sacred with the associations of centuries, "Veni Creator Spiritus." As these words, which the Church in all ages has used on holy occasions, were begun by those on the foremost vessel, the sound floated to the next where it was taken up and then the next continued it, so that soon from all the ships rose the solemn, prayerful chant, in which the strong voices of manhood blended with the silvery tones of children, and formed a harmony that was wafted away to the hills by the willing breeze.[1]

While this hymn was still sounding on the air, and the hearts of all were full of contending emotions, "the sailors set their sails in the name of God." The white wings filled at once and sought to set the vessels free. Another moment of pause and then, at a common signal, the anchors were raised from their rocky beds. The ships began to move. With none of the noisy circumstances of these days of steamers but silently gliding, they sought the mouth of the harbor without interrupting the music, which still rose on the air. In quiet stateliness, they passed beneath the lofty rock of Nôtre Dame de la Garde, from which looked down on them, as it does today, the Chapel of the Sailors, and immediately the crisp waves and the fresh breeze and the boundless horizon told the little voyagers that they were at sea!

The crowds sought the cliffs that they might watch the seven vessels until they disappeared. How eagerly did they look who had once been numbered with the army! As now they saw the ships bounding gladly over the waters, the sails bellying with the health-giving wind, and the oriflammes and banners waving so brilliantly, and as they heard the shouts of exultation and the songs of triumph which their former companions uttered, more than one regretted his retreat and would gladly have rejoined the band that seemed really destined to win fame and honor. But they sadly felt that it was too late and that now they must commence again the weary and tedious march back to their distant and inglorious homes, where they would have

[1] This hymn was always sung on such occasions. *Vide* Joinville.

to bear the shame of hearing tidings of the progress of an enterprise from which they had cravenly withdrawn.

Behold then the citizens and the timid children watching the receding ships. Soon the songs grow indistinct, as they come over the water—then they become inaudible. After that the flags and banners still tell of hope and of joy, until their colors are invisible. The day draws to its close, and when, upon the blue hills of the east there fall the bright rays of the setting sun, the ships which bear the precious burdens are far away and seem as seven white birds nestling on the deep for the slumber of night. Then over all creeps the twilight, and the watchers on the shore return to the city, casting a longing look after the pilgrims, as they had often done before, after other and older ones.

Darkness then comes on, and in its sable folds covers the land and the sea and envelops the seven ships that were sailing away with the five thousand little pilgrims to seek the land of Israel.

CHAPTER VIII

The Tidings From Beyond the Sea

I

The Long Suspense

When the seven ships sailed away into that August night they were not heard of again for eighteen long years.

After that several months had elapsed and the time had come when tidings of their arrival in Palestine should reach France, each returning Crusader, or pilgrim, or merchant was asked if he had any news of the children who had embarked to seek the Holy Land. To all these inquiries the reply was given that no such fleet had been heard of in any port. As weeks passed by, the anxiety increased, and every ship was eagerly expected to bring the news, but yet none could give the hoped-for answer. Still the anxious trusted that the delay was due to contrary winds, or to the children having disembarked in Sicily or Rhodes to rest, and that they would yet laugh at their fears, when some welcome bark brought the story of arrival and of victory. A year passed away, and another, until all hope died, and they who had treasures on the missing vessels resigned themselves to the belief that beneath the waters their dear ones lay, overwhelmed in some disastrous storm.

The succeeding years were stirring ones. The strife between Otho and Frederick for the crown of Germany was ended by the triumph of the latter, who began his splendid reign in his southern home at Naples, where he gathered the most elegant court which had yet been seen in Europe. But Innocent, who had raised him, found that he could not rule him; and, after years of strife, he had to compromise with him at last in

1230. In England, the misfortunes of John continued. His barons made him sign the Magna Charta in 1215, and then Innocent, with whose claims this document conflicted, found himself obliged to turn and uphold the king whom he had so lately sought to crush, in order that John might be able to break loose from the engagement. Thus, beaten about by the Pope and his subjects, the poor man died, broken-hearted. Henry III ascended the throne, and his reign, during the period with which we are concerned, was peaceful.

But above all was Europe excited by the resuscitation of interest in the Crusades. Innocent, finding his previous measures vain, had summoned the Lateran Council in order to awaken the Church to its duty. At this great assembly from all parts of Christendom, the Pontiff urged in plaintive or in threatening tones, as suited him, the sorrowful condition of the Christians in Palestine and the hopeless state of the cause. He appealed to them to avenge the slain, to put an end to the sufferings of those pining in prisons, or in slavery, and to deliver the holy places now weeping under the footsteps of the heathen. His endeavors succeeded. The Council granted him all the aid he asked, passed the measures he proposed, and the sixth Crusade was ordered. It was so diligently and effectually preached that, in 1217, the largest army was gathered which had ever taken the Cross, and, under Andrew, King of Hungary, departed from Spalatro and Brundusium. The peculiar feature of this Crusade was that, while the interest in the cause was less than usual among the nobility, among the people it was greater, and they rushed to enlist, indignant at the apathy of their superiors. The fleets reached Ptolemais in safety and were welcomed as liberating angels by the beleaguered Christians. Hopes long dormant were revived, and again was it expected that the King of Jerusalem would, from his throne in that city, rule the redeemed land. But these hopes were soon to be dashed by the weak conduct of Andrew, who became discouraged in the hour of

success and returned to Europe with half of his troops. As
trophies, he took with him the head of Peter, the right hand of
Thomas, and one of the seven "waterpots" in which the wine
was made at Cana. This treasure comforted him, and, as he
said, rewarded his trust in its efficacy, for at once a dangerous
conspiracy was suppressed when he reached his dominions with
these relics. Yet, as other bands of Crusaders from the northern
parts of Europe arrived afterwards, the armies in Palestine were
still formidable. At this time, however, the resolve was made
to seek a new road to Jerusalem by breaking the Mohammedan
power in another quarter. Accordingly, they all embarked for
Egypt, and in April, 1218, after a siege of several months, had
gained only part of the defenses of Damietta, when most of
the army, weary and discouraged by the desperate resistance
which they met, returned home with no fruits of their valor.
But others who came from southern Europe as these departed
maintained the siege for a year and a half, enduring all forms
of suffering. At last, finding that no beleaguering could starve
the defenders into a surrender, an assault was ordered, when to
the horror of the Christians, they found defenseless walls
around a deserted city. Of the seventy thousand Moslems who
had entered there to uphold their cause, only three thousand
remained, who looked more like specters than men. This was
one of the most brilliant crises of the Crusades. The Mohammedans now offered full possession of the Holy Land if the
Christians would abandon Egypt. But in the flush of victory
these terms were foolishly rejected, and they demanded the
wealth of the latter to minister to the glory of the former.
The Saracens refused to yield any more and renewed the war,
the result of which was that soon they were so victorious that
the decimated and famished Crusaders were glad to ask permission to embark and return to Europe.

After an interval of several years, Frederick of Germany at
last undertook his long contemplated Crusade. He had made

the promise to the Pope, but now being under excommunication was forbidden to carry it out, and actually had to encounter a prohibition addressed to all the world against aiding him. But he persisted and gained splendid success. Within a year he had so humbled the Sultan that a treaty was granted, by which a truce of ten years was declared, and the possession of Jerusalem freely made over to the Christians. The Emperor signalized his triumph there by his coronation. The affairs of his dominions calling him home, the Christians were left in 1229 by this, the most romantic of the Crusades, dwelling securely again in the city which had been the object of so many prayers, so many tears, and so many wars.

These were the events which intervened between the departure of the army of children from Marseilles, and the date at which we again take up the thread of their story.

During all these vicissitudes, and the attendant excitement throughout Europe, the events of 1212 grew remote, and the children were forgotten by the nations who had seen and suffered so much in the interval. Yet they were not forgotten by all, for that strange Crusade was ever in the minds of many a noble and of many a peasant of France.

They who had been members of the army of Stephen, but who had returned from Marseilles, did not forget their companions, whose fate was involved in obscurity. As had been the case with the Germans, they were held to their vows by the Pope, and commanded to redeem their promise to fight for the sacred cause when they reached maturer years; only those were exempted who were too young to comprehend the nature of a vow or too aged to be of any service in the army. Many of these were in the ranks which fought at Damietta and fell there or returned wiser men. When they had abandoned the enterprise at Marseilles, they regretted for a while that they had not possessed enough endurance to persevere. But as time flew by, and no tidings came of glory nor even of the fate of those who had sailed on the seven vessels, and as the different ways in which they might have perished were considered, they rejoiced at their return and compassionated those whom they once had envied.

And the five thousand were also remembered by many a stricken household, and many a tear was called forth by the recollection of their departure. As long as there was any chance, hope lingered, but when year after year had passed away and there had come no tidings, it vanished, and all hearts yielded to the conviction that the bed of the sea had become the unknelled and uncoffined sepulchre of those who had expected to make it their triumphant pathway. The people of Marseilles remembered too the seven vessels that had departed from their port with their novel burdens but that had never reached their destination, and they were wont to speak of and muse upon the mystery of their fate. Porcus and Ferreus were objects of sympathy, it may be, for their disinterestedness which had cost them so much. But they asked no reward or sympathy when so great a calamity as the destruction of the children overshadowed their lesser misfortune.

During the progress of the Crusades which had occurred since 1212, it was natural to suppose that those expeditions would lead to a solution of the mystery, and efforts were probably made by them to ascertain the fate of the children. But all was in vain. Victory was enjoyed and defeat experienced, but no light was shed upon the sad question.

Eighteen years thus passed without any tidings from beyond the sea or any clue as to the fate of the five thousand children. The day of judgment alone, it was believed, would raise the veil from the sad mystery.

The year 1230 had come, and the cloud which enveloped the strange story was as dark as ever, when one day an aged priest arrived in Europe and said that he was one of those who had sailed from Marseilles in 1212 and that he was able to tell the result of the enterprise. The news spread through France and Germany, and all hearts were thrilled, as from home to home the report flew that the long-mourned little ones had been heard from, that one of their company had returned. Let us now take up the narrative where we dropped it, and continue it, as related by the priest, whose tale is preserved by several chroniclers, but principally by one old monk who dwelt in Liège.[1]

II

The Departure from Marseilles

If they who from the mouth of the harbor watched the receding vessels on that day of parting had strange thoughts passing through their minds, more peculiar were the emotions experienced by those who, sailing out upon the great and mysterious deep, saw the land becoming hourly more remote and more indistinct. At first the flush of hope drew shouts and songs from all, but soon more than one face was wet with tears, as they realized that strange and sorrowful vicissitudes might have to be encountered before they should again greet those retreating shores. They felt that they might yet have to share the captivity and death of those whom they had enlisted to avenge. The leaders sought diligently to banish all such gloomy thoughts, by promises of glory and reminding them of God's evident favor. They spoke of a brief and pleasant voyage over the beautiful sea, by many a lovely island on which all fruits grew, to the land made sacred by the memories of Jesus and of Mary, and where they were to reap the honors which kings and nobles and mailed men had failed to win. This may have succeeded for a while, but as the day advanced, the children could not be kept from despondent musings on the perils of

---

[1] The priest's story is preserved by *Albericus,* the *Magnum Chron. Belgicum,* *Roger Bacon,* and *Thomas de Champré.*

the sea. The terrors associated with it in those days of superstition and of ignorance cannot be appreciated by us, in whose time it seems so nearly conquered. Each pilgrim, or sailor, or Crusader who crossed it brought home many wonderful stories, which were readily believed by the credulous, and all were credulous then. Priest and layman, noble and peasant lived equally under a craven fear of the supernatural. By those whose minds were so full of fables, the ordinary phenomena of nature were transformed into miracles of God or wonders of Satan, and every voyage added to the stock of tales which were current as to the terrors of the deep. The chronicles of medieval times are full of them, when they refer to the sea at all. One writer tells us that "in that part of the Mediterranean which lies by the coast of Africa, the water is always boiling on account of the great heat, and that consequently there are no fishes," of course implying that navigation is not pleasant there. Another tells us that in some parts of the same coast "the sea is higher than the land, and it seemeth that it would cover the earth, and yet it passeth not its bounds. And in this land, whoso turneth himself toward the East, the shadow of himself is on the right side, and here in our country the shadow is on the left side." The peculiar reason for assigning these strange features to the coast of Africa was that, owing to dread of the Mohammedans who peopled it, the Christian sailors dared not approach it, and where they could not discover by investigation, imagination was always busy in filling up the unknown regions, very much as human nature is prone to do even now.

Another traveler tells us of "a great, round mountain" which they met with at sea one Saturday at vesper time. Having passed it, they made all sail during the night, and as their fancy peopled it with "griffons," Saracens, and other disagreeable inhabitants, they desired to leave it behind as rapidly as possible. But in the morning, when they supposed it "fifty leagues astern," they were dismayed at beholding it fearfully near. In terror lest the dwellers on this remarkable island should capture them and put them to death, at the recommendation of "a discreet churchman," the passengers sought, by religious ceremonies, to dissolve the spell which either kept the vessel still, or else drew the mountain after it. Processions with litanies were made around the masts of the ship, and soon, to their joy, it receded rapidly. The narrator, in simplicity, and apparently to shift the responsibility for the story, adds that during this time he was below, terribly seasick. The phenomenon of the Fata Morgana was not understood and very naturally plays a prominent part among the wonders of the sea. Pilgrims often tell us of its freaks. They say that before them they would see a beautiful expanse with gardens and groves, among which were stately edifices and dazzling palaces, forming a scene of rare luxuriance all resting upon the waters and fading away on either side into nothingness. In wonder the mariners would sail towards the shore, and when it seemed that their course was about to lie through fields and flowers, all would vanish in a twinkling, leaving the unrelieved waste of waters.

In consequence of such stories, the real perils were those the least dreaded. Saints could not be relied on against such things as phantom ships, and mighty spirits which appeared in the storm, or against ravishing sights and sounds which treacherously led the unwary to the hidden reefs, or "single waves of towering size" that were sometimes to be seen rolling alone over the sea, or winds that often lifted vessels out of the water. Yet the people also feared the ordinary dangers of the deep and with reason. The vessels were comparatively frail; they were scarcely manageable in a storm, and navigation was little understood. Hardly a fleet is reported to have crossed the Mediterranean without a large part of the ships being lost in one way or another, and rarely were any of the passengers or of the crew rescued, because there were no proper means to that end.

All these and other perils were, of course, familiar by report to the children whose fortunes we are following, and an excited memory brought them up as the hills of France grew indistinct and the twilight came on. Wistfully did they watch the coast until no longer discernible, and as darkness descended there were many hearts which regretted the decision to persevere in the Crusade. But even the most anxious became weary, and eyes which had been strained to peer through the dimness were tired and readily closed in sleep. Side by side, the seven vessels sailed through the night before the favoring breeze, gently rising and falling on the billows, while their living cargoes slumbering within them forgot, in the pleasures of dreamland, their regrets and their fears.

The morning came and found the ships making good progress on their course, with the dark and rocky coast of Corsica in the distance on their left hand. This day closed, and the second evening after their departure the vessels were sailing by the southern extremity of that rugged island. A few more such days, said the little ones, and we will reach the Holy Land. Alas! they knew not what the morrow was to reveal!

III
The Shipwreck on the Isle of Falcons, or San Pietro

Clustered around the southwestern extremity of the island of Sardinia lies a group of smaller islands, which were well known to the ancients, as they lay in the much traveled route between Gaul and Greece, Italy, or Egypt. As adventurous Greeks had passed them, far back in the twilight of history, they noticed that the largest and the most westward of them was frequented by flocks of falcons. In view of this they gave it the name of Hierakon, which in later times was translated into the Latin equivalent, Accipitrum, both meaning the island of Falcons. When this latter language had passed away, and

Italian had taken its place, we find that the name it bore was San Pietro, by which it is still called. It is probable, as has been suggested, that this was a mere corruption of the Latin, for the words resemble each other in sound, and the former designation could easily glide into the latter, especially among those who loved to call all places after saints, and to whom such an opportunity to honor Peter was too good to be lost.

This island, two or three miles long, terminates to the northward in an abrupt and high cliff. Thence it slopes away to the southward and ends in a plain that inclines gently to the sea. Its surface being barren and destitute of fresh water, it has not been inhabited until recently, except that in summer fishermen made it their temporary place of sojourn, while they caught the tunnies which abound in the surrounding waters. But they only enlivened the scene for a few weeks, and after that the ashes of their fires alone remained to tell that man had trodden its silent shores.

Yet, in the long history of the island, it had known a brief period when it was not entirely uninhabited. In days which are remote and unrecorded, some man, disgusted with the world, had made there his abode. He did not dwell actually on the main island, but upon a smaller one which is severed from it by a chasm—a mere rock in comparison—but which, seen from certain directions, seems as one with it. It may be that he fled hither from the scenes of pillage which were witnessed when the northern barbarians overran Italy, or that, when religion had sunk as low as the once proud city of Caesar had fallen, his heart longed for purer associations and deliverance from scenes of temptation and of hypocrisy. Whatever it was that impelled this unnamed man, he knew that only in solitude could he worship God in freedom—only in some remote spot could he escape the miseries of the age. And it may have been that, as he had on some journey been musing on this longing of his heart, he passed by this lonely isle whose solitude and beauty met his desires, so that he chose it as his home and fixed on the small islet by its side for the erection of his hut.

There through the years he dwelt, and from the high cliffs where the fresh winds brought exhilaration and associations of purity, he looked forth over the magnificent waters to where they met the sky and found food for ceaseless meditation in contemplating their ever varying appearance. When the storm was abroad he watched its fury, and then, when it was subdued, he beheld the foam-streaked waves settle to rest again beneath the returned sunlight. And from scenes like these, his thoughts wandered forth to that land beyond the sunset and beyond the clouds where weary mortals rest, and of which he read in the vision of Patmos, which was congenial to him, written by another exile on a lonely rock that "there shall be no more sea." When, day by day, the vessels passed in the offing to and from the busy marts of commerce, he thought of the life he had left, of which they were suggestive reminders, not to wish he were again in its scenes but to rejoice that he was free from its cares, its perils, and its sins. The fishermen, as they came each summer, used to see him standing by his little hut or sitting on some rocky eminence, and they returned to tell strange stories of the solitary inhabitant of that barren island, while he found pleasure in listening to their melodious songs, which were borne to his ears as they dried their nets on the shore. Time rolled on; the seasons came and went until he died in his loneliness, and the waters he had learned to love sounded a dirge around his desolate sepulchre. When the next summer arrived, the returning fishermen missed him in his accustomed places, and they knew that on some wild, cold day of winter the mysterious recluse had gone away from the world which had afforded him so unenviable a home.

And thus he came and passed away, but the place of his dwelling was remembered and his story perpetuated, for fishermen were wont to point out to their comrades from age to age the Hermit's Rock lying beneath the cliffs of San Pietro.

When last we saw the children on the seven ships, the second evening of their voyage was approaching, and they were about passing from the coast of Corsica to that of Sardinia. The night passed away, and when the morning came, they saw on their left hand the mountains and bays of the latter island. Their progress had therefore been so rapid that all augured well for a speedy passage to Palestine. But that day was to blight their hopes. For a storm arose, and in its power tossed the vessels about like toys, bringing to the children's hearts dismay and misery. As the hours elapsed, their sufferings and terror increased, for, as we have seen, the primitive build of the ships and the undeveloped state of navigation rendered a tempest a fearful thing beyond what we can now appreciate. Huddled together below the decks, the little Crusaders heard the waves strike blows upon the frail planks, which threatened each moment to yield, and they were thrown from side to side as the vessels pitched and rolled. Whatever elation they may have felt at the prospect of reaching the goal of their enterprise now died away, and their fears, their sickness, and their bruises drew forth ejaculations of distress and prayers for mercy, which were smothered by the roaring winds ere they had wandered far from the staggering barks. The scene on each vessel may easily be imagined, where several hundred children were crowded, expecting momentarily to be engulfed in the sea. The priests who had accompanied them, if they sought to administer consolation, told of the promise of the Church that they who died in the cause of the Cross should enter at once upon eternal blessedness and be sure of a complete forgiveness; that they might meet their death in the storm or in the battle: either was, for such as they, a portal opening directly into Paradise. They said that, in that world of bliss, they might stand side by side with the heroes who had fallen on the blood-stained fields of

Palestine, though their feet had never trodden those plains. But words were vain to these terrified children. They dreaded death in the angry sea. At length, as the unmanageable ships drove on, they came in sight of the island of San Pietro, looming up before them in the mist. Here was a faint hope! If they could weather that point, before them was an open sea where they could run before the wind, with no fear of reefs or rocks. The vessels had become scattered in the storm, and it was evident that some of them could avoid the island, while others were too far to leeward. How anxiously did they see the island become nearer and nearer! It soon became manifest that at least two of the ships were doomed—that they were drifting irresistibly toward the great white breakers, which seemed exulting at the prospect of the fair prey that they were soon to grasp and to dash to pieces in their remorseless sport. The minutes passed in awful suspense. Those on the five vessels which were to escape beheld with anguish the approaching fate of their comrades. Swiftly they drifted on towards their dreadful end. At last they were close to that rock which was washed by the spray, beneath the high cliffs of San Pietro, and over which the falcons hovered and screamed. There was a moment of pause between the final billows. That moment passed, and the next wave tossed them among the breakers. The shrieks and prayers of the perishing rose in agony on the air. Wave after wave washed them off the decks. A few more blows broke the hulks in pieces, and then all cries were silenced in the waters.

When the storm had ended and the darkness had gone, the returning sunlight fell on broken timbers and splintered spars and beheld the subsiding seas tossing to and fro among the wet rocks the pale and mangled corpses of more than a thousand children.

And so, in the twelve hundred and twelfth year of grace, were two ships, laden with fair and hopeful youths of France

who had taken the Cross under the guidance of Stephen,
wrecked in a wild storm at the foot of the Hermit's Rock.

IV

The Captives of Bujeiah

About one hundred miles east of the city of Algiers, the sailor
finds the best harbor on the Mediterranean coast of Africa,
where in case of storm he may have that safe and pleasant
anchorage which Alexandria and others more famous cannot
provide. It runs obliquely into the land, and the winds and
waves of the sea are shut out by an elevated, narrow promontory, which forms a splendid breakwater of a mile in length,
in the lee of which there is always a calm. And as the mariner
lies there at anchor, waiting for the tempest without to cease,
he is struck by the picturesque beauty of the scenery around
him. To the south and westward rise lofty mountains, one
behind another until lost in the distance, and they are of so
great an altitude that snow rests on them until June, although
the climate is tropical. Their slopes and the valleys between are
covered with luxuriant groves of cypress and fig trees, chestnuts
and olives, while down to the shore come yellow fields of barley
and arbors laden with purple grapes. In the corner, where the
promontory juts out from the mainland, looking across the gulf
toward the mountains, extensive and ancient walls enclose a
vast, luxuriant orchard, and through its dense foliage peep out
the white houses and turrets of the city of Bujeiah. Above this
there rises the hill of Gouraya, beautifully terraced to the elevation of two thousand feet, and as it were guarding the town
which nestles at its base.[1]

Those walls, so entirely disproportioned to the population

[1] For descriptions of Bujeiah as it was and as it is, see Rozet, Shaw, Dureau
de la Malle, and other travelers in Algeria and Kabylia; also Condé's *Arabs in
Spain*, chap. XLII. It is because wax candles were once imported in great quantities from this place that the French called them "Bougies," which is the French
name of the city.

they now contain, indicate a past of greater prosperity and tell the beholder that once there was a vast city where the orchards grow. The feature of a safe harbor, so rare on that inhospitable coast, made this a commercial point at an early period. The Carthaginians founded here an important colony, called Saldae, which continued to flourish after Rome had conquered and absorbed the possessions of her rival. When Rome in turn fell before conquerors, Saldae declined and almost disappeared. When the Saracens became masters of this part of Africa, they saw the value of the position, and a new city rose on the ruins of the old one which was called Bedschijah, or Bujeiah. In the twelfth century it was the capital of a large kingdom, whose sovereigns were independent of the caliphs and ruled from Tunis to Gibraltar. But in 1151, Abdelraumen, who governed the Saracens in Spain, subdued this kingdom, and at the time of the Children's Crusade, it remained subject to his successors. It was now in its glory, having within its walls over one hundred thousand inhabitants. It was, next to Cairo, the principal city in Africa and possessed a lucrative and extensive commerce. The writers of the time dwell fondly on its beauty, telling us that in the splendor of its edifices and the wealth and luxury of its people, it excelled, as it probably did at the time, any place on the Mediterranean. The Mohammedans of all lands acknowledged it to be one of the holy cities, and gave it the name of "Little Mecca." To this place, in this its era of power and beauty, does our story take us now.

The children on the five ships had sorrowfully seen their unfortunate comrades drifting toward the breakers. It may be they had lost sight of them before they struck, or they may have even witnessed the dreadful catastrophe. At any rate, they felt that they were safe themselves when the threatening headland was weathered. When the storm ceased they were grateful for deliverance from the perils which had surrounded them, while hope revived that they would yet reach the port they sought. They counted the days to elapse and began to imagine the scenes of welcome which awaited them.

But that hope was only revived to be more cruelly blighted. They now learned that they were victims of an infamous treachery, and we are to follow them, not to the Holy Land, but to slavery among the Saracens. We learn, to our dismay, from the returned priest that Hugo Porcus and William Ferreus, the kind and disinterested merchants of Marseilles, were simply slave dealers and that they had contracted to sell these confiding children to the Mohammedans, to whom such a consignment would be of rare value, to minister to their luxury. Thus was explained the remarkable readiness of these men to furnish vessels gratuitously, and the hypocrisy of professing to do it all *causa Dei absque pretio* exposed, but, alas, when too late! How the victims learned their betrayal we do not know. It may have been when Saracen vessels came in sight, and, surrounding them, separated the ships, making the sailors steer as they ordered; or it may be that they were removed from the vessels of Marseilles and carried to those of the enemy, on which they were to be conveyed whither their captors chose. Whatever was the event which revealed the treachery of the merchants, never has the sea beheld a sadder moment than when these thousands of children became aware that they were slaves to the Mohammedans. For all knew what that lot implied. In every village of Europe had some escaped or liberated captive told the story of his slavery, and by additions of his own to facts which, unimproved, were terrible enough, made that fate proverbially horrible. We can therefore easily picture the feelings of the young pilgrims when they discovered that in that bondage, the description of which had always made them shudder, they were to pass their lives. They looked around upon the sea but found none to help. The limitless expanse told them that they were completely at the mercy of that race whom they had learned to hate and fear from earliest infancy.

During their lamentations they were separated, and while part were carried towards Alexandria, the rest were conveyed to Bujeiah by their captors. Following these we soon reach this harbor and behold the final destination of this fragment of the hosts which we saw depart from Vendôme.

Very beautiful was the view presented as one entered the bay of Bujeiah in 1212. The city covered the flank of the Gouraya, built on terraces, where dark and luxuriant verdure almost hid the houses and seemed to try to conceal also the high and slender minarets, while the blue sky and scented breezes told of a voluptuous climate. The fields and valleys around were assiduously cultivated and revealed a teeming and prosperous population, which was also proved by the masts of many vessels riding safely at anchor. There was no scene so fair from the Pillars of Hercules to the River of Egypt, although now few know that it ever existed. But to the children, these beauties had no power to charm. They knew that before them was a life of labor in the service of those whom they had been taught to despise and for whose extermination they had been taught to pray. Among scenes so fair and landscapes so lovely, they were to be slaves in a hopeless slavery.

The vessels came to, the sails were furled, the anchors dropped, and the voyage, begun in Marseilles, was at length ended. But how differently from their hopes! "Was it for this," said they, "that we have taken the Cross and enlisted in the army of Christ? Is it thus the soldiers of the holy cause are rewarded? Has God's arm been shortened that it cannot save?"

They were taken ashore and dispersed, as they who bought them wished, and then their servitude began! To their respective homes we cannot follow them. Scattered over the neighboring territory and throughout the city, they found their lot eased or hardened by cruel or kinder masters, or according to the nature of the work allotted to them. And so they entered upon their menial tasks, while the friends whom they had left in distant France supposed they were reaping glory in rescuing the Sepulchre and restoring the fallen kingdom of Jerusalem. They soon saw how vain it was for them to look for rescue or ransom. They felt that the tidings of their fate had not reached their kindred and that long since they had been given up as dead. How did they wish that word could be sent to the distant dear ones, that their condition might at least be known if it could not be changed! But the winds would bear no message, nor did the waves as they broke bring any news from the far-off shore whence they had rolled, regardless of whether Christian or heathen owned the coast whereon they dashed. In course of time the children grew up to manhood and age crept over them, finding them still slaves. Now and then they probably met with other captives taken in the wars, or on the sea, and from them heard of their homes. They learned of the Crusades undertaken since their departure, of the successes achieved and of the failures experienced, and then the old men wept at their tasks as they thought how much more enviable it would have been to have perished in some hour of victory on the holy soil of Palestine.

One by one the captives died, some by disease, some by cruelty; others pined away in old age. At length all had dropped their weary burdens, and their toils and sorrows ended. The betrayed Crusaders slept the sleep which liberates from the oppressor's yoke and rested in the land where the voice of the taskmaster is not heard.

They all died in slavery. Not one of the many hundreds ever saw Europe again.[1]

One hundred years later, this same Bujeiah was the scene of the martyrdom of one whose labors and death have invested the place with interest as great as that associated with the memory of these children.

Raymond Lully spent a large part of his life in this city, preaching among enemies and in fearlessness of peril the

---

[1] Albericus; Hecker.

Gospel of Christ. This man, one of the most remarkable of the Middle Ages, will forever stand in the front rank of the army of missionaries; for truly like the Master was he who could, in the midst of the Crusades, proclaim everywhere, "The Holy Land can be won in no other way than as thou, O Lord Jesus Christ, and thy Apostles won it, by love, by prayers, by shedding of tears and of blood." And it was here, in this scene of the young Crusader's servitude, that he was stoned to death by the Mohammedans in 1314.

Bujeiah has long since fallen. Its natural beauties are unchanged. The foliage is as green, the fruits as luscious, the sky as blue as when the betrayed little ones labored there and pined. But a few broken columns and illegible inscriptions are all that remain of the once proud edifices of a great and luxurious city.

It is now in the possession of the French, and people from the land of the children bear rule where the children were captives. But few of those who have made it their home for purposes of business think that with the soil they tread there is mingled the dust of these youths of their own fair France, who died there seven centuries ago.

v

Alexandria and Bagdad

Having seen the fate of the children on the vessels which were taken to Bujeiah, we turn to follow those from whom they were separated. They were also destined never to see their homes again. The port to which they were to be taken was Alexandria, nearly fifteen hundred miles distant from San Pietro. Long and tedious was the voyage, giving them painfully ample time to realize their condition, and meditate on the future before them. Suffering in body and in mind, they sailed along the inhospitable coast of Africa, until at length they saw a faint line of sand hills, in front of which rose the two solitary columns, Cleopatra's Needle and Pompey's Pillar, which then, as now, formed the landmarks for the mariner on

that monotonous shore and indicated the site of Alexandria.
This once great city was at this time sunk to the lowest point
that it reached between its grandeur in ancient times and its
revival in modern days. It had gradually declined after the fall
of the Roman Empire, but the conquest by the Saracens in the
tenth century and the building of Cairo completed its humilia-
tion. In 1212 it was a mere port of the latter city, containing a
few hovels, where a scanty and miserable population dwelt
among noble ruins which told of the ages when it had rivaled
Rome in size, and eclipsed it in luxury and wealth. The superior
beauty of its situation, as well as the residence of the Sultan,
made Cairo rise at the cost of the older city, so that soon it
seemed that the site of the capital of the Ptolemies, and the
abode of Mark and of Cyril, was to be tenantless, and that
desolation was to reign in it as supreme as it had before the
conqueror of Darius ordered its construction, to perpetuate his
name, and constitute his sepulchral monument.

Past the ruins of the fallen Pharos the children were carried
into the deserted harbor, and perhaps to some broken column
on the Hepta-stadium their captors made fast the ships.

When landed, they were sold and dispersed. Bitter were the
tears, heartrending the partings, as their purchasers tore them
from each other, and they bade farewell with that intensity
which they feel who never expect to meet again on earth.

A great many of the children were bought on the spot by
the Governor of Alexandria, Maschemuth, and were destined
to lead a miserable life in cultivating his lands and in menial
services about his dwelling, for he is said to have been a cruel
master.

The ecclesiastics were more fortunate who had accompanied
the little Crusaders, whether with the good intention of caring
for and advising them, or, as was more probable, because they
were carried away by the prevailing excitement. Here, for the
first time, we learn how considerable was their number. We are
told that the Sultan of Egypt, or the Caliph,[1] as he is errone-

ously called by chroniclers, "bought four hundred clerks, among whom were eighty priests." This Sultan was Malek Kamel, son of the usurper Malek Adel, better known as the famous Saphadin, who was still alive but had abdicated and divided his vast empire among his sons, with whom he lived. One chronicler tells us that this Malek Adel was the son of the great Saladin, and that he had studied twenty-three years in Paris, during which time he had mastered all the languages of Europe, and that even on his throne he still wore his university robe, while he had ceased to offer, as Mohammedans were believed to do, camel's flesh in sacrifice. The whole story is evidently a fiction, for instead of his being the son of Saladin, his father had dethroned and killed Saladin's son, Al Aziz. As regards his studying in Paris, the relations existing between the adherents of the two religions would have prevented it, if his father had been capable of permitting so unique an occurrence.

Thus, while we cannot believe this story, although some have not thought it impossible, nevertheless his conduct in regard to the ecclesiastics whom he purchased of the slave dealers shows us remarkable traits of character for one circumstanced as he was. His selection was one which awakens our surprise, as does his treatment of them afterwards. He took them to Cairo and kept them in a merely nominal slavery in that beautiful and luxurious city. They dwelt by themselves in his palace, and their only duties were teaching him, and whom else he chose, the letters of Europe. Their yoke was as easy as a yoke could ever be, and in learned pursuits they passed their time, possessing all they wished, save their liberty.

In another direction are we taken, as we follow the fate of the other children besides those brought by the Caliph and Maschemuth. They fell into the hands of masters who, to sell them the better, prepared to take them to far distant Bagdad. Their route lay across the Delta of the Nile, then over the

---

[1] Albericus.

weary desert to Palestine, and into that Holy Land where they had hoped to march as conquerors, they were brought as captives. With what emotions did they behold the walls of the sacred city, for whose conquest they had enlisted, but which now was only a stopping place on the path to bondage! Theirs was not the privilege to worship by a liberated Sepulchre. They may have seen the dome which covered it, from the khan where their captors kept them, only to know it was inaccessible and defiled by the custody of heathen. Thus sadly was fulfilled the hope they had often expressed, as on their march to Marseilles they had sung "Our feet shall stand within thy walls, O Jerusalem!"

But their owners hurried them away. Past Nazareth and Hattin, the scene of the disastrous defeat of the Crusaders, past the dark waters of Galilee and over the mountains, they were dragged towards Damascus. The beauty which here enchants the traveler had no power to please them, and it was without the regret he feels that they saw its minarets and domes and lovely foliage disappear, when, leaving it, they penetrated the desert on their eastward journey. Then ensued that dreadful march across the wide waste which stretches unrelieved from Syria to Mesopotamia. Once was the monotony of sand broken, as they tarried to encamp among the solitary ruins of Palmyra, where the moon then, as today, looked down on no sleepers save the Bedouins or the caravans that make its deserted streets their resting place. But these ruins also disappeared behind the desert horizon, and one day, as at sea, was like another, sad, long, and unrelieved, until after several weeks, the weary camels gladly drank of the waters of the Euphrates. They were transported down the river for a few days, and then, leaving it and crossing the intervening plains, they reached the city they sought, on the banks of the Tigris. Here their journeyings were ended. For this had they assumed the Cross a few short months ago! This was the destination where the pilgrimage, begun by the Loire or the Seine, was to terminate! Since the year, now nearly closed, had commenced, how much had they seen! How far had they traveled! How much had they endured! It must have seemed, in view of the rapidity with which the events had succeeded each other, as a horrid dream since, yesterday as it were, they had parted from their kindred in far distant France.

They were now dispersed, as each purchaser took to his home those whom he selected. According to the character of the various masters was the hardship of their servitude. The city was, as Cairo, extremely luxurious and beautiful, being the theme of poets for its splendor. Here resided the great chief of the Moslems, the Caliph, and the wealth of many lands was made to minister to their common capital. But though the children found here refinement and comfort which France or Europe could not equal, they thought wistfully of their ruder homes, far away to the westward, and during the long years of bondage, they longed to see once again their native villages and their beloved friends.

There is some definite light cast on the lot of a few, which brings us to the last scene, and it is a scene of martyrdom. Not long after the arrival of these captives, there was held a meeting of Saracen princes in Bagdad.[1] The object of it is not told us. It was probably for consultation, in view of the distracted state of the Mohammedan world; for, at the time, there were many dissensions among the turbulent and aspiring sultans of the different provinces, and the once compact empire was divided and apparently in danger of self-destruction. Whatever was the reason for this gathering, the princes agreed in one thing—enmity to the Christians; and when they learned of the presence of the children who had vainly enlisted as Crusaders, they considered its becoming the capital of "the chief of all the faithful," and a proper object for so august an assembly, to endeavor to convert these young unbelievers. Into their presence some of the children were brought. Every art was used to win

---

[1] Albericus says this was in the same year with their departure.

them. Entreaty, argument, and threat were employed to lead them to adopt the creed of the Prophet. They were promised the sensual delights of the believers, and all the comforts that that city could provide, if they would yield; while, on the other hand, death by torture and agony would be the result of obstinacy. But temptations could not move them; threats could not intimidate them. Though before such powerful sovereigns, they remained steadfast, and children of tender age baffled all the wiles of these rulers of Asia. When their determination was evident, some were ordered to be put to death, in the expectation that the spectacle might affect the rest; but the survivors were still firm, and the enraged Saracens commanded that others should be executed, until their vengeance was gratified, or until they judged it wiser to let the rest live, in the hope that time might do what threats could not effect. Before their thirst for blood was satisfied, eighteen were put to death, by the bowstring or by drowning.

Where is there a scene in history more touching than the martyrdom of these eighteen little ones, whom all the power and state of the Caliph and his princes could neither tempt nor dismay? How noble a termination of their Crusade! How much more illustrious is their memory for this faithfulness than any victories in battle or subjugation of enemies could have rendered it!

These children, who died rather than gain a life of ease by denying their Lord, remind us of others, who on the banks of the same river in days long previous had manifested equal firmness. By that Tigris had the captive children of Israel been enslaved, and their tears had mingled with the waters which now were turgid with the Crusaders' blood. There did the latter, like their predecessors, not forget Jerusalem, neither did they cease to cling to their faith at the cost of their "chief joy." Like them did the tortured and betrayed little ones "speak of the Lord's testimonies even before princes, and were not ashamed"; and with the remains of those who could not for their sorrows "sing the Lord's song in a strange land," lie mingled the now indistinguishable dust of those who only dared in concealment to pray the prayers they had learned in their unforgotten homes beyond the desert and beyond the sea. As the sufferings of the former exiles expiated many sins which caused God to let the Assyrians "carry them away captive," thus does the constancy of these whose fate we have seen make us forget their folly, and it atones for their disobedience to the parents whose wisdom they now confessed in tears. Such deaths cover, to human eyes, the imperfections and spots in the lives of those who meet them.

Strange is it that Bujeiah and Bagdad are each rendered memorable by two separate testimonies to God's truth in bondage and death!

VI
Conclusion of the Story of the French Children

The martyrdom of the eighteen children in Bagdad occurred, as was stated, in the same year in which they had left their homes. It must have been in the ensuing winter.

Concerning the fate of the rest who were taken to that distant region, we know no more. That single scene of bloodshed and cruelty alone has been recorded. They lived and labored, grew old and died by the banks of the Tigris and of the Euphrates, waiting in vain for the day of liberation; hearing, it may be, as did those in Bujeiah, of the disasters or of the successes of the Christian Crusaders, but feeling that no victory could bring relief to them.

As years passed away, hopes grew feebler, and, at last, they resigned themselves to the sad belief that they were forgotten or deemed by their friends to have perished. In Egypt, we saw that there were a number who dwelt in Cairo and many in Alexandria. Those in the former city continued in their easy slavery and found in their companionship some consolation for their exile. The priest who returned was one of these. The

Sultan had liberated him, but we do not know why. Whatever was the reason, it was an act of precious moment to those in Europe who first heard from him of the fate of the ships which had departed from Marseilles eighteen years before, and of the thousands they had carried. He said that, after these intervening years, the ecclesiastics in Cairo were still as kindly treated and had as their only occupation literary pursuits.

It was stated that Maschemuth, governor of Alexandria, had purchased a large number of the children on their arrival. The returned priest said that there were still living at the time of his release seven hundred of these, now, of course, having attained the age of manhood.

One fact related by this priest concerning the children ends his story. He said that he had never heard of a single one of the Crusaders, old or young, who had abandoned the faith of their home and of their infancy. There may have been others exposed to persecution than those in Bagdad; many were subject to countless strong temptations to adopt the easy, sensuous faith of their masters, but they resisted threats and wiles unto the end. It is true that the sphere of knowledge of this priest was but partial, yet those for whom he could speak positively were as much liable to apostasy as any, and consequently, when he says that he never heard that one abandoned Christianity, it is enough to show that this faithfulness was general. The earnest were too pious to become heathen. They who had undertaken the Crusade for other motives were led by their perils to find their comfort in the faith they had once neglected.

The effect of the promulgation of these tidings by the priest can be more easily imagined than described. It revived interest in a theme which had become almost forgotten.

Many a question did he have to answer, addressed by anxious parents, and few were the cases where he could give to the bereaved the welcome reply that their "Joseph" was "still alive and in Egypt."

Of course, with their interest in the news, the people also expressed their indignation at the conduct of the merchants, Porcus and Ferreus. But, as we shall see, they were not yet to receive their due reward.

Efforts may have been made to secure the liberation of the Crusaders that still lived, but in vain, for none ever returned. They lingered on in servitude in their various places of abode through passing years. They may have heard of the violent and many political changes of the Mohammedan world, but these did not help them; they only changed their masters. Those who lived until twenty years after the priest's return, when Saint Louis waged his war in Egypt, may have thought that this would end in their deliverance. But it was in vain that they looked to this. How anxiously must they have heard or seen the conflicts between their brethren and their oppressors!

When this Crusade was ended in 1250, the last chance had vanished, for nothing occurred afterwards which could help them or that might free them.

And so, without hope, the scattered captives worked at their tasks in the various regions whither they had been carried, forgetting the tongue of their infancy, but not forgetting its scenes, experiencing the vicissitudes which resulted from the caprices of their masters, until all was over. The last straggler in the rear of the dissolving band escaped from slavery by the great gateway to liberty, and at length the morning dawned when the muezzin's cry from airy tower calling the faithful to prayer was heard no longer by any of those whose fortunes we have followed to their mournful close.

Was ever a journey as sad as that one? We have seen an army which left Vendôme so full of hope under their youthful leader, betrayed, scattered, and enslaved. They had indeed found a way through the sea, but the price of their passage was their life and their freedom. Some of them reached Jerusalem, but they walked its streets as captives and looked upon Olivet in chains.

CHAPTER IX

The Fate of the Leaders
and of the Betrayers

It remains for us, in closing, to gather up the hints that are preserved regarding the three youths who led the children, that, as we have seen "from the towns and cities of all countries, ran with eager steps to the parts beyond the sea," and concerning those who betrayed them so basely.

As regards Stephen, Roger de Wendover says that "an infinite number followed the aforesaid master to the Mediterranean," but rather shows his ignorance of the details of the transaction and of the state of affairs in Palestine by adding, "crossing which, they went on their way, singing in orderly procession and in troops." We cannot feel certain from so general a statement that Stephen retained his influence until they reached Marseilles, and yet it is not improbable. The journey was not long, though tedious while it lasted, and with him were many others who were interested in continuing his authority from reasons of a selfish character. He may have really led them into the city they sought. After that we know no more about him. We cannot tell whether or not he embarked on the ships of the merchants and shared the fate of his victims in shipwreck or slavery. It may be that he returned to Cloyes and there passed succeeding years in tending the sheep he had left to conduct an army and that, in quiet hours on the hillsides about his home, he mused in afterdays on that summer dream of glory.

Concerning Nicholas we know that he was the leader of his

band when they entered Genoa, for two eyewitnesses record the fact.[1] But this is the last that we hear of him.

Whether he remained there is not stated. It may be that he was of those who concluded to make there their home or that he persevered to Rome. That he did not return to Cologne seems apparent from one fact which is recorded. It is said that when the people of that city learned the fate of the children and the story of their sufferings, they revenged the little ones by hanging his father.[2] This would lead us to infer that they could not lay hold of Nicholas, or they would have visited their indignation also upon him, for they would have sooner identified him with the deceivers than with the deceived. It also shows that his father played a prominent part in originating the Crusade and aimed at his own advantage.

His colleague is not spoken of in the chronicles by name. We only are told that the other army had a leader. Who he was or what became of him cannot now be discovered.

One other leader to whom we referred has been more fortunate in the extent to which his fame has been preserved. We saw that in northern France a man of mature years, Jacob of Hungary, preached the Crusade of Stephen and led many children to Vendôme. He is not mentioned again in connection with the movement. We do not know if he accompanied the band to Marseilles or left it when on the way thither.

But he comes forward again in history and as a prominent actor in a transaction of a nature similar to this of which we are treating.

Seasons passed away, and the sad year of 1250 came, when the vast army of Saint Louis had been dispersed on the shores of the Mediterranean and the King himself made prisoner. A general feeling of despondency spread over France, and the people were brokenhearted by the captivity of their beloved sovereign. Then, in some way which cannot be traced, a feeling

[1] Caffari and Sicardi.
[2] *Gesta Trevirorum.*

arose that the cause of the Crusaders was to be made victorious by means of the shepherds, and it spread as rapidly as had the idea in 1212 that the children were to render it triumphant. Here Jacob of Hungary comes to the surface again. He was now an old man, with a long, white beard and the aspect of a prophet and had spent the intervening years as a shepherd. He preached in all the towns of France and Flanders that he was commissioned by God to lead an army of peasants to rescue the Holy Land and liberate the King. Soon he found himself at the head of more than a hundred thousand enthusiastic "Pastors," as they called themselves, and they started to seek the way to Palestine. But they soon found that they might use their power more advantageously to themselves nearer home, and they declaimed no longer against the Saracens but against the Church, the rulers, and the rich. Pillaging and robbing as they went, they resolved to assemble at Bourges, where Jacob was to perform miracles and where he was to rule as a king. But by this time the people were aroused and united to oppose the rabble. They met them at Villeneuve, and, in a sanguinary battle, routed the Pastors beyond all possibility of reassembling. Jacob of Hungary was killed by a soldier in the conflict, who with his axe finished the old man's career by cutting off his head. So terminated the strange story of this twice successful deceiver.[1]

If our sympathies were awakened by the sad fate which befell the children who formed the French army in this strange Crusade, our indignation must have been equally aroused at the peculiarly cruel treachery of the merchants, who played upon their ignorance and their confidence in order to betray them.

It is with satisfaction that we learn that they did not go unpunished, but that they met with justice although for another crime.

Whether they fled from Marseilles in order to escape the

---

[1] Roger de Wendover and Roger Bacon.

vengeance which they dreaded or left that city for other reasons, we are not told, but they appear again upon another field of action, and in the prosecution of an undertaking similar to this one in which we have seen them, but, happily, not with equal success.

Frederick II, Emperor of Germany, was also King of Sicily. This beautiful and fertile island had been wrested from the Saracens by Guiscard in 1090, but the latter never ceased to desire to regain it, or to make frequent desperate attempts to that end. These efforts continued up to the date of which we are speaking. At the time, the Mohammedans had a slight foothold upon the island, when they sought by a new plan to secure it altogether. That was to capture the Emperor. The opportunity to do this was afforded by the frequent visits which he made to this part of his dominions, to attend to its wants and to promote that administration of justice for which his reign was conspicuous.

The Emir Mirabel, ruler of the Saracens in Sicily, conceived this plan and found ready agents in the merchants, Porcus and Ferreus, who probably had been in relation with him in their old trade of selling Christians into slavery. The agreement was made that they should seek to capture Frederick alive, or, if this could not be accomplished, to assassinate him. But, carefully as they laid their schemes, the vigilance of the Emperor was too great for them. The plot was discovered, and Mirabel with his two sons and the merchants were made prisoners. In such a case punishment was summary and severe. The five, though the heathen were far less guilty than their treacherous assistants, were all hung upon one gallows, and we leave them hanging there, not sorry that the martyrs of San Pietro, Bujeiah, Alexandria, and Bagdad were avenged.[1]

We have now traced from its commencement to its sad termination a movement which is unique in the varied history

[1] Albericus.

of the world and the wildest delusion of an age of delusions.[1]

Sixty thousand families, it is estimated, were by it saddened or bereaved, and in its mad current nearly a hundred thousand children were carried away to hardships or to death. Of this number at least a third never saw again the homes whence the songs and banners had lured them. They died by the banks of every stream and on every hillside along the routes of the three armies, some while seeking the distant sea, others while wearily seeking their homes. Others still, as we have seen, sailed from Pisa, Brindisi, and Marseilles to die in shipwreck and in slavery.

And most extraordinary is the briefness of the space of time within which it was all comprehended. Eight short months comprised it, from the call of Stephen among his flocks by Cloyes to the scene of martyrdom in distant Bagdad. Within this short period, the great throb of child-life rose and ceased, its work complete. We can scarcely believe that all transpired so rapidly, but this rests upon distinct assertions of the authorities.

It was stated that the cruel delusion was the work of the emissaries of Rome who, despairing of arousing Europe to a new interest in the Crusades, thought such a movement, for which they found the children ready, owing to the arts and appeals, to which their elders were accustomed, would conduce to the result which they sought to effect. They succeeded probably better than they had intended and awoke a spirit which they could not, if they would, suppress. For the deception the Pope had no words of rebuke, for its progress no syllables of prohibition, for the victims no tears of sympathy. He was not a man to be influenced by sentiments of a tender nature, and he saw in this an auxiliary to his great desire. We noticed the cruelty with which he decreed that the children must renew the attempt to rescue Palestine when older and redeem the

---

[1] Appendix A.

vows which they had taken. In keeping with this conduct was a remark which has been preserved, uttered by him when endeavoring to raise a new crusade: "These boys shame us, for, while they rush to the recovery of the Holy Land, we sleep." [1] It resulted then, as we saw, that this fatal and delusive undertaking furnished an argument wherewith to appeal to the adults. And this man's assumed name was Innocent. His original name was Lothario, Count of Segno.

One more consideration occurs to us, which is the illustration which this strange Crusade affords us of the unsettled state of Europe in these times. We are apt to rise from perusal of medieval history with a strong, yet vague idea of disorder and unrest, lawlessness and anarchy. But the vast difference between society now and what it was then is manifested in new vividness when we think what the condition of affairs must have been, in order that it could have been possible for such an affair as this to occur, or that which soon followed, the ravages of the Pastors. Demoralization so complete makes one grateful that his lot has been cast in these latter days, whose turmoils and disorders seem as tranquillity itself, compared with the life which our ancestors led. They were romantic days, as they are called, but the pen of the novelist or poet has endued them with a halo which would surprise those who lived in them and found them to be days of want, of trouble, and of struggle. They were sadly commonplace to the generations who had to endure them.

But we now must turn to the last part of our task, the description of the monument of the shipwrecked children, which is also the sole relic of the entire transaction.

---

[1] Albert Stadensis quotes the Pope's language.

CHAPTER X

Ecclesia Novorum Innocentium

I
The Church

When the sad tidings of the fate of the children that left Marseilles became known, as we have seen, by the return of the liberated priest eighteen years later, the reigning Pope, Gregory IX, resolved to erect a tribute to the memory of those who were victims of the ambition or the zeal of his predecessor. There was one place eminently appropriate for such a structure —the island of San Pietro, where it would serve to recall the event in the scene of one of its most touching episodes, and which was, moreover, the only place of the many where they had met their deaths which was not inaccessible to Christians.

Many of the bodies had been washed ashore, after that fatal storm, and some kind hands had gathered and buried them on the lonely island. During the intervening years they had lain there, but they were now to have a more appropriate resting place. The Pope caused a church to be built, and the remains of the little ones were placed within it. It was to be both their memorial and their shrine. With touching and beautiful reference to the murdered children of Bethlehem, this monument over the remains of youths who died, as they thought, in Christ's cause, was called, ECCLESIA NOVORUM INNOCENTIUM; *the Church of the New Innocents*. Rarely has a name been given to a church more appropriate, or more replete with suggestiveness.

In order that services might be maintained in so sacred a spot and that the structure might be cared for where there was no population to attend to it, the Pope endowed the church sufficiently to support twelve prebends, who were to form the only inhabitants of the isle and to continue the sounds of prayer and praise from day to day and from year to year.

But they were not destined to be as lonely as they may have anticipated. In an age of pilgrimages and of holy places, a spot like this would not remain unvisited. It soon became a favorite shrine, and from the islands around crowds came to utter eager prayers or to fulfill the vows of superstition. The blue waters bore on their bosom many a boat, laden with pilgrims, who, as they approached the shore, heard the music of the services that was wafted towards them by the breeze. It became the noted place of that part of the Mediterranean and was looked upon with reverence as a "Holy Isle," where the wonderful children slept, whose intercession was most precious in view of their virtues and their martyrdom.

Thus did years pass away, and generation after generation came to worship where their ancestors had prayed. Three centuries after its erection we hear of the church again. Alberic tells us that it was then as much frequented as ever, and that the story of the children was listened to with undiminished interest. This interest was also increased by the priests, in that they showed to the pilgrims the bodies of the shipwrecked Crusaders, still entire and undecayed, which was a perpetual miracle to encourage the faithful in their prayers and stimulate their liberality. This succeeded, for it was comparatively a small tax upon the credulity of the happy mortals who lived in the regretted ages when all was believed, and no questions were asked.

After this glimpse, which Alberic gives us, we lose sight of the church, and it is no more mentioned in historic records. How long a time priests and pilgrims continued to pray there we know not. But probably before many years, various causes led to its being deserted. As the turmoils and excitements of the succeeding ages came on, or as other shrines rose into favor, the interest in the sepulchre of the children whose story was now so old naturally waned, and the number of the visitors to the island decreased. When the prebends found their occupation gone and the offerings scanty and rare, they desisted from their thankless duties and departed. On some day that is unrecorded, the last mass was sung, the last taper extinguished, and the lonely priests sought the boat that was to bear them away, leaving to silence and desertion the scene of three centuries of pilgrimage and prayer.

When thus abandoned and uncared for, the church soon became dilapidated. In that exposed situation the storms of winter told with annually increasing effect and the work of ruin made rapid progress. The decayed and beaten roof gave way at length and left the edifice open to the sunlight and the rain. Vines clambered up the crumbling walls and waved their branches in the open windows, while growing mosses beautified the wreck. Weeds choked up the once thronged portal, and obliterated the long-trodden pathway, while in the silent grass-grown aisle and around the falling altar, wild animals played undisturbed.

Thus were the children left to slumber on in their neglected and deserted tomb; but the little birds that found there a nest and a home sang over them sweeter, purer requiems than ever had been chanted by forgotten priests.

II
The Ruin

The island that had again become deserted and silent remained so until five hundred years after the shipwreck of the children, but we do not know how long after the abandonment of their shrine, when, for the first time in its history, it became peopled, and its scanty fields received cultivation.

In 1737, a party of Christian captives held in slavery in

Tabarca, on the coast of Africa, succeeded in effecting their escape, under the leadership of one Tagliafico, whom they selected as their chief. Sailing northwards, across the sea, they reached San Pietro and resolved to colonize it. Being encouraged by the King of Sardinia, the colony grew rapidly in numbers and wealth, profiting by the valuable fisheries in the vicinity, and the precious deposits of coral which were not too deep to escape the search of the adventurous divers of the island. In course of time the population has reached the number of ten thousand, who dwell mostly in the little city of Carlo Forte, whose white houses may be seen from far over the sea, nestled close to the shore beneath the shadow of the mountains which form the northern end of the island. They contain a happy, peaceful people, as is shown by the fact, recorded by a traveler who visited them in 1828, that there had never been a lawsuit among them during the ninety years of their history that had elapsed. When the fugitives landed in 1737, they found upon the island the remains of the Church of the New Innocents, which filled them with astonishment, as they knew that they were the first inhabitants of the isle. Being able to find no clue to its origin, they regarded it as a thing of mystery and often talked to one another about that desolate edifice which they had discovered where, as they supposed, before them man had never dwelt. When strangers visited San Pietro, they were shown this relic, but no one could conjecture its history. In the beginning of this century an English traveler, wandering among the islands of the Mediterranean, reached this one. He tells us that the wonder of the people was as great as ever, and that they were wont to assert that the island had been named after this church by their fathers when they landed. He knew no more himself and seems to indorse the story. But the next generation forgot all about the edifice itself; and, of late years, anyone who would have asked to be conducted to the ruined church would have been told that there was no such thing to be found on the island, even by those most familiar with its surface and its history. So completely has the memory of the children perished that the people who dwell on San Pietro know not that their monument and their shrine is among them, that close to their homes are the remains of the edifice where for centuries prayers were said above their sepulchre, and a spot which has been sought by the feet of throngs of pilgrims. Within that silent enclosure many a shepherd has slept, little dreaming of those young Crusaders who lay buried there; and many children have played in this falling structure without suspecting that it was the memorial of a touching story of the betrayal and death of hundreds like themselves of a long past age.

But let us, in closing, describe this relic around which our interest centers.[1] It stands upon an eminence behind the city of Carlo Forte and overlooks a large part of San Pietro, while from it may be seen the rocky and high outlines of the island of Sardinia beyond the sparkling waters of the strait. The church was originally quadrangular, with a steep, peaked roof. In the eastern end was the altar and over it a window, the entrance being from the westward. But the front face has fallen down and leaves but the rear and sides remaining, and these latter are crumbling away. There are no signs of the roof; if there was a tower, it has disappeared. All is deserted and grass-grown within. The stones of which the walls are built are of irregular size, and put in place without having been carefully dressed, while around the ruin the turf is thickly strewn with those that have fallen. Near by are two deep and ancient wells, which were probably excavated when the church was built, for the use of the priests and the pilgrims, and not far distant catacombs have been discovered, which may have been the resting places for those who died there during the

[1] Appendix B.

period when the sanctity of the spot made it an abode of men, between the two epochs of its loneliness.

There it stands, weather-beaten and gray, between the mountains and the water, a neglected monument of a forgotten tragedy! May the hand of time deal gently with it, and the strong-armed ivy, clambering over its stones, long hold them together in its firm grasp! The sepulchres of Godfrey, of Baldwin, of Richard, and of other Crusaders are honored by many a visitor; but lonely and unfrequented is this tomb of those who, having entered on the same great cause with more unselfish motives, found their deaths in the horrors of the storm, a tomb which recalls all of our now finished story of the most touching and romantic episode of that struggle which convulsed and excited the world during more than two hundred years.

For here our task is ended. We conclude the narrative of the event which we have sought to rescue from the oblivion into which it had fallen, with our gaze resting upon the only relic of it which we possess, the one memorial which has survived the lapse of centuries. The closing scene is a ruined church, looking out over the blue sea, and within its crumbling walls the shipwrecked children are still sleeping.

Appendices

APPENDIX A

This movement has not been entirely unique in kind, though it was quite so in degree.

Two events in subsequent years resembled it. The first is recorded by Marten Crusius, in his "Annales Suevici," Fol. LVII. Part III. p. 405, and also in the chronicle of the Monastery of Elwangen. The second is related by John Lindner, of Pirna, in his "Excerpta." I quote the narration of them in Hecker's *Child-pilgrimages,* a rare work, translated and issued in England by the Sydenham Society.

"It ('the excitement of the world of children') was confined to the city of Erfurt, and was very transient, but not the less presents all the distinctive marks of a religious disease, and was more so than other pilgrimages, as far at least as has come down to posterity. On the fifteenth of July, 1237, there assembled, unknown to their parents, more than a thousand children, who left by the Löber gate, and wandered, dancing and leaping, by the Steigerwald, to Arnstadt. A congress, such as this, as if by agreement, resembles an instinctive impulse, as in animals, when, for instance, storks and swallows assemble for their migration; the same phenomenon has doubtless taken place in all child-pilgrimages; it was also remarked by eye-witnesses of the first of them, in a manner characteristic of the Middle Ages. It was not until the next day that the parents learned the occurrence, and they fetched the children back in carts. No one could say who had enticed them away. Many of them are said to have continued ill some time after, and, in particular, to have suffered from trembling of the limbs; perhaps also from convulsions. The whole affair is obscure, and so little an account has been taken of it by contemporaries that the chronicles only speak of the fact and say nothing of its causes. The only probable conjecture is that the festivities connected with the canonization of St. Elizabeth, the Landgravine of Thuringia, had excited, in the child-world of Erfurt, this itch for devotion, which sought to relieve itself by displays of spinal activity, for this child-pilgrimage is in very near proximity to the dancing mania.

"Still more obscure is a child-pilgrimage of 1458, of which the motives were clearly religious. It is probably, at present, almost impossible to trace the chain of ideas which occasioned it; it is enough that it was in honor of the Archangel Michael. More than one hundred children, from Hall in Suabia, set out against the will of their parents for Mont St. Michel, in Normandy. They could not, by any means, be restrained; and if force was employed, they fell severely ill, and some even died. The mayor, unable to prevent the journey, kindly furnished them a guide for the long distance and an ass to carry their luggage. They are said to have actually reached the then world-renowned abbey, now, as is well known, a state prison, and to have performed their devotions there. We have absolutely no other information of them."

Who, that has been at this wonderful St. Michael's Mount, near Avranches, can fail to be impressed by the scene of these children marching across the wide expanse of beach to seek it, where it rises as a fretted pyramid, at high tide an inaccessible island, nearly three miles from the shore? It is of all spots in Europe probably the most surrounded by curious and vivid associations of a legendary and historical nature. It is not now a state prison, having been given to the Bishop of Avranches.

APPENDIX B

As the discovery of the ruins of this church is rather interesting I have thought it worth relating.

When compiling this book, having discovered that such an edifice had been erected, I naturally desired to know if any ruins remained, and supposed that its loneliness would have tended to its preservation. After a long search for some description of the island, an account of a visit to San Pietro was found in Smythe's "Travels in Sardinia," published in London in 1828. To my gratification, I found that he said that its present appellation is derived from a little old chapel near the town (Carlo Forte), the date of which is unknown, it having been found in a ruined state when the colony arrived. No other account of this ruin could be found, and I therefore took steps to secure a further description of it, presuming it to be the Church of the New Innocents, for reasons given below.

A letter to the polite Curé of Carlo Forte brought a reply from him that there was no such edifice on the island as that which I told him Smythe had seen.

Then, through my father, who was in Italy, my friend, Mr. Newton Perkins, an art student, was persuaded to go to the island, which he kindly did. The following letter tells his story and shows the extent to which the ruin had become forgotten.

CAGLIARI, ISLAND OF SARDINIA,
March 18, 1867.

REV. MR. GRAY:

MY DEAR SIR,—I have just returned from a trip to the Island of San Pietro, where I have been to look for the chapel known to have been erected by Pope Gregory IX to commemorate the shipwreck of vessels, near that spot, containing young Crusaders. I left Leghorn in a steamer on the evening of the 12th of March, and after a pleasant sail of thirty-eight hours arrived at Cagliari, the largest town in the Island of Sardinia, being a place of some 28,000 inhabitants. I spent one day and night at Cagliari, and while there called on the English Consul. I found him a very agreeable old gentleman, and derived some information from him about my present business. On the morning of Friday the 15th, I started in an open carriage for a ride across the southern portion of the island, to the village of Iglesias, a small town on the western coast. I had with me an intelligent Sard, who acted as guide. We rode all day, stopping occasionally for refreshment at some dirty little village or settlement on our route. The houses were built of clay-baked brick, held together by straw, the ends of which could be clearly seen where the bricks had been cut in two. About six in the evening I arrived at Iglesias, and called upon an Englishman, the superintendent of a company of miners working in that neighborhood. Through the kindness of the superintendent (whose name, I regret to say, has slipped by mind) I was provided with letters of introduction to several persons, which were of great service. On the morning of the 16th March, I started quite early for a drive over the mountain to the shore of the western coast. After reaching the summit of Mount Sirai, I had a fine view of the two islands lying before me. San Pietro is the more northern one, quite high and precipitous at the northern extremity, and gradually sloping towards the sea at the southern part. San Antiocho is larger in size, but not so thickly populated. In this island excavations are in progress, and many valuable relics have been discovered. About nine o'clock I arrived at a little fishermen's village, called Portoscuro, but so small and insignificant as not to be noted on any map I had seen. I was unfortunate in missing the boat at this point, and had to wait several hours for its return. About eleven o'clock, however, I started in a sail boat from Portoscuro for San Pietro. An hour's sail brought me to Carlo Forte, the only settlement on the Island of San Pietro. It is a small town, and, what is quite a rarity in this country, the houses look clean, are whitewashed, and numbered on the outside. The town is surrounded by a wall, and surmounted by a fortress. At a distance the appearance of the town is quite pleasing. The white houses, the gray walls and fortress, and the tall white spire of the church, make quite a striking contrast. A few fishermen's boats were lying at the wharf, and the lazy beggars were sunning themselves, lying on the hard cobble-stones, as we approached. Having landed, I went to the residence of the French Consul, Mr. Romby, to whom I had a letter of introduction. He received me very kindly. But now the object of my mission seemed to be an absurd one. When I mentioned that there probably were the ruins of a church on the island, erected in the thirteenth century, people shook their heads. There were two churches, indeed, one called a cathedral; but one was wooden, and had a spire; the other, a dingy-looking stone building, with a cracked bell. Mr. Romby, however, very politely walked out with me about the island, and explained all that he could of the history of the churches then existing. Outside the wall, however, nearly a mile from the shore, we came upon the ruins of something, either a house or a church. The gentleman said it had been there ever since he had lived on the island. He knew not, and had never cared to inquire, what it originally was. This, he said, was the only ruin on the island, except an old Roman wall and two deep wells, both of which we examined. At some distance from this spot were the remains of an old catacomb. Thinking that possibly this might be the ruins I was in search of, I made two sketches of it for you, that you might consider the matter yourself. There are reasons why this might have been the church known as the *"Ecclesia Novorum Innocentium."* First, Because it stood entirely by itself, no habitation being within twenty rods of it and is on a slight eminence. Second, The building faces directly east, if we may consider the standing wall as the place of the altar; and this is probable, as it had a high window, and no door. Third, The stones were quite large and irregular at the base, and smaller as they approached the top. Fourth, It had not the appearance of having been restored, since the ground was strewed with stones and *débris.*

The inhabitants of the island are a mixture of the Genoese and Italians. Coral fishery and the catching of the tunny are the chief employments of the men: the women cultivate the fields. Northward from the Island of San Pietro are two smaller islands, which from the shores of Sardinia appear to be but parts of the island itself. On these islands are several houses; and here are the peculiar nets placed for catching the tunnies, which are taken in the summer months only.

I regret that I cannot give you a photograph of the island or its buildings. I was promised some by a brother of the consul, who was an amateur photographer, but never received them.

This is about all the information I can give you of the Island of San Pietro and the Church of the New Innocents. I was obliged to return that same afternoon to Iglesias, and could not spend more time on the island.

Very truly yours,

NEWTON PERKINS.

It will be seen that Mr. Perkins thinks that the edifice he saw was the Church of the New Innocents. The argument seems so conclusive that I have not hesitated in claiming that it was. It is briefly thus:

Three hundred years ago, in the middle of the sixteenth century, Albericus said that the church was still standing, and still resorted to as a shrine. It continued to be so for some time after, we do not know how long, but let us allow fifty years. Therefore the church was entire, up to about 1600.

After this, there were no inhabitants upon San Pietro until 1737, when the colonists under Tagliafico landed. Yet they find, upon landing, a church and wonder at it, on an uninhabited island. What they found must have been that which was standing in 1600, for there was no population in the interval to build any edifices, and there never had been any before, except those sent by the Pope to erect the monument and shrine of the children.

Now, Smythe saw the same edifice that the colonists found; he was there fifty years ago, and the people pointed it out to him as having been discovered by Tagliafico and his followers, and as having, as they supposed, given the name to the island. He saw this structure when it was less dilapidated than now and says it was a church. Furthermore, the edifice of which Mr. Perkins speaks is the same one that Smythe describes, and thus all the links seem found to identify this lonely ruin with the Church of the New Innocents, built six hundred years ago.

Concerning
George Zabriskie Gray

GEORGE ZABRISKIE GRAY, D.D.

A MEMORIAL SERMON

PREACHED AT

ST. JOHN'S MEMORIAL CHURCH

CAMBRIDGE, MASSACHUSETTS,

ON THE

FEAST OF ALL SAINTS

NOVEMBER 1, 1889,

BY THE

REV. WILLIAM LAWRENCE

PRINTED FOR THE FAMILY

MDCCCXC

SOURCE: *Biography*, Volume Gon-Gut, New York Public Library (35-page pamphlet)

Sermon

Thou shalt give him everlasting felicity, and make him glad with the joy of Thy countenance. *Psalm 21:6.*

Two or three years ago, when Dr. Gray was preparing a sermon to preach in the Chapel of Harvard University, he exclaimed in his decided way: "Those young men do not want arguments, but a life." Then laying aside all thought of a labored discourse, he told the students, in clear and simple language, the story of Bishop Hannington's life and martyrdom.

After his example I bring to you, on this evening of the Feast of All Saints, simply the story of a consecrated life; and I leave it with you to speak for itself and for Christ.

The ancestry of George Zabriskie Gray * foretells the man. On his mother's side the ancient Polish blood had intermingled with that of the French Huguenot and the Scotch and Dutch Protestant. Since his Dutch-Huguenot ancestor landed in America, about two hundred years ago, a large number of ministers can trace their descent to him, and today there are more than a score of them preaching the Gospel. On his father's side, also, we find a stock of Presbyterians who emigrated to Ireland during Cromwell's Protectorate, came to this country in 1795, and settled on the Hudson, near Newburgh. They there revealed the characteristics of the country gentleman, with tastes

* 1838–1889.

[177]

for art and verse, tempered, however, in the last generation, by a life of mercantile energy.

When then we learn that a child was born in New York on the fourteenth day of July, 1838, of such parentage, and that he was baptized in the Broome Street Reformed Dutch Church by the name of George Zabriskie, thus bearing with his surname the stamp of both sides of the house, we know what a manner of man to expect. We look for a piety of decided traits molding a life of intellectual and administrative development, and we are not disappointed in our expectations. Other features were revealed in passing years, but these were his fundamental characteristics.

During his childhood the last trait mentioned, that of administrative development, could be trusted to take care of itself in New York, where the conversation on business in the home, the restless industry of the street, and the growing realization of the city as the metropolis kept the boy alert to the practical interests of life.

There was but little danger of any check of intellectual development; for a boy born with an insatiable hunger for books and knowledge can be trusted to find intellectual stimulus.

But amidst the distractions of a restless, city life piety must have a hard struggle for existence, unless the pressure of the world is held at arm's length by the sanctity of a religious home. This, which he always felt to be the greatest of blessings, was given him. His religious impressions were also being unconsciously affected by the worship of the University Place Church which his family attended during his boyhood. Its pastor, the Rev. Dr. Potts, a strong Presbyterian—who at a New England dinner provoked a controversy with Bishop Wainwright by the toast, "a Church without a Bishop and a State without a King"—was hardly the man to lead one towards the Episcopal Church. Yet there was in the semi-Gothic architecture of the building, the style of music and the pastor's solemn and stately manner of conducting the service, an ancient and ecclesiastical atmosphere which distinguished this from most Presbyterian churches of that day.

While he was at school in Geneva, Switzerland, the influence of the Lutheran Service and that of the English Chapel must have deepened his interest in our church, so that when his family moved to Staten Island, and in the absence of a Presbyterian Church, connected themselves with St. John's Church, Clifton, the influence of the life and teachings of the Rev. Dr. John C. Eccleston led both Zabriskie and his brother Albert to be confirmed in the church in which they were to do noble work, and where their names will be treasured as saints, diverse in character but one in Christ.

After four years in the University of New York, from which he was graduated in 1858, his horizon began to widen. His school experience in Geneva had already brought him into contact with boys of varied classes and nationalities, but a journey to Europe, Egypt, and the Holy Land in 1859 developed new features.

It was then that he began to realize that love of traveling which became almost a passion with him, a passion, however, held in close check by his sense of duty to his work as Pastor and Dean.

In reading books of travels, in waylaying travelers from New Zealand, India, China, Japan, and Alaska, in planning anticipated journeys which never took place, in a quick run to Mexico, Florida, or Bermuda and occasionally to Europe, he tasted the pleasures which in their fullness fidelity to his calling denied him.

At this time, too, he tested his ability to catch foreign languages. Through his Genevan life, French and German were almost as familiar to him as his mother tongue. As he and his fellow-travelers passed through various countries, he was so quick to catch and use the vernacular that he became their interpreter.

Upon his return he entered the seminary at Alexandria. The school was then in its glory. Dr. Sparrow, the Nestor of Evangelical Theology, was great in character and teaching; his fellow-students, some of whom now stand as leaders in the church, were congenial; and the atmosphere of the place was in harmony with his religious opinions. In the evangelical spirit of these earlier leaders, who then taught at Alexandria and gave their impress to the school, in their personal piety, their prayerful spirit, and their strong theology, there was a noble basis for the wider thought and life of this generation. However far we may have moved from them in method, we may be ever grateful for their spiritual leadership, for there is no movement or school of thought in the Church of England or this country during the past fifty years but must trace much of its spiritual heritage to the piety of evangelicalism before it was touched by the deadly poison of partisanship.

On the twenty-second of April, 1862, George Zabriskie Gray was presented to Bishop Horatio Potter to be ordained.

As he stands before the chancel in St. Luke's Church, Catskill, we see a young man twenty-four years of age, of strong physique, high intellectual attainments, fond of books, society, and travel, with marked business capacity and with exceptional opportunities to exercise them and build up a large fortune. He could have taken a high position in the city of his birth as merchant, banker, or lawyer; he might have passed his days in devotion to literature or travel, and at the same time have held the respect of all persons as a gentleman and a Christian. On the other hand, there was the calling of the Christian minister. It offered no other inducement than that of preaching the Gospel of his Lord and Saviour, the daily routine of the parish priest in visiting the sick and afflicted, and perhaps the

bearing his part in elevating the literary and theological stand-
ards in the church.

There was no hesitation in his decision. With no consciousness that he was making any great sacrifice, he simply acted
according to the dictates of his conscience and consecrated himself, his strength, intellectual capacities, and his fortune in the
service of the Master. To the Bishop's question, "Do you trust
that you are inwardly moved by the Holy Ghost to take upon
you this Office and Ministration, to serve God for the promoting of His glory, and the edifying of His people," he gave his
glad reply in that strong tone with which we are so familiar,
"I trust so," and he never for a moment regretted it.

While such decisions are made and such consecrations occur,
the mouth of the cynic who says that religion and the ministry
have ceased to appeal to the devotion of strong and able men
is stopped. For if there ever was a man, virile in all his features, it was Dr. Gray.

A few months later he entered by marriage into that union
which, next to his ministry, gave him the greatest joy and
comfort.

It was not in him to rest on the eve of action. Immediately
after his ordination he threw himself into parish work. First
for a few months in charge of the two churches at Warwick,
N.Y., and Vernon, N.J., then for two years at Kinderhook,
N.Y., and again for eleven years at Bergen Point, N.J., he
was a devoted pastor, priest, and preacher.

No man knows his own characteristic capacities for the holy
ministry until he has tested them. It is wonderful how the work
develops and reveals the latent powers. That there was behind
his strong voice and frame, his brusque and sometimes aggressive manner a heart as tender as a child's may not have surprised his nearest friends, but was a perpetual revelation to
everyone who came to know him well. Some have thought that
this manner, which belied his character, was the result of a

pushing executive mind which chafed at delay, others that it was due to his nervous temperament. Probably both are partly right. But some of his nearest friends have felt that the habit was gained in early years through his effort to conceal his tender heart. His emotional nature was very near the surface; to have given it full play would have weakened him; therefore he unconsciously covered it with this thin shell of an abrupt manner, which, however, in the face of trouble or sorrow was so easily shattered.

The people of his three parishes, as well as the congregation of this chapel, quickly discovered his tender sympathy. To be unfortunate, to be sick or afflicted was an immediate call upon him. He carried his people's cares with him day and night. Among the poor as well as the rich at Bergen Point his memory is still tenderly cherished. His sympathy and love for children was also intensified by the death of his first-born son.

One class, those who, once living in wealth or comfort, had fallen into straightened circumstances, he seemed to take as his peculiar charge. He gave them money and sympathy; but, what is more rare, he made them feel that his house was their second home. Pastoral work was always natural and dear to him.

The combination of these characteristics made him the able preacher that he was. His executive ability and taste for business kept him in touch with practical life, his interest in men led him to wish to tell them what had been revealed to him; the flash of light from a fresh text was a thought for himself, but no sooner his than he burned to give it to others. His immense range of reading and his wide experience in traveling illustrated and illumined his thought. With a good degree of imagination, with a voice as strong and dogmatic as that of the Baptist, he could warn and rebuke; with a heart tender and full of pity for sinning, suffering men, he could plead and comfort. "The comfortable Gospel" was a favorite phrase of his. The tones of his voice still ring in my ears as from this pulpit in behalf of his people he echoed the prayer of the Psalmist, "Lead me to the Rock that is higher than I." Every thought and experience inwrought into his character was the storehouse of his sermons; he spoke with the power of personal conviction and personal faith. And when in the deep distress of his last days, he was tasting as he never had before the comfort and the hope of a loving Saviour, he exclaimed, "If God should give me my strength again, how I could preach." And how he would have preached!

Anyone who knew him knows that his parish work was aggressive. He led his people in charities and missionary activities. His cottage lectures, still remembered at Bergen Point, have borne fruit in the erection of St. John's Church.

Two features in this part of his life should not be passed without notice. These were the years when partisan spirit in the church was at its height. The Episcopal Church was thought to be large enough for only one school of churchmanship, and each was striving for the mastery. Voices like that of Muhlenberg were heard, but, like the prophet's, were unheeded. We now look back on those days with sorrow tinged with perhaps a supercilious sense of our present superiority. But the leaders on both or all sides were strong and wise men in their day. It is always easy for the generation who reap the fruits of a battle to criticize the plans or strategy of the actors.

It was only to be expected that a man who was of warm temperament and active brain, and who had in his veins the blood of French Huguenots and Dutch Presbyterians, should speak strongly and act vigorously. As the Diocese of New Jersey had little sympathy with the evangelical element, the voice of young Gray, though often heard in the din of the battle, was little regarded. But let this stand as characteristic of the man, that many of his best and dearest friends were on the other side. No differences of opinion could weaken the cords of his affection. He was incapable of harboring ill-will, and though his Bishop, Odenheimer, differed with him on ecclesiastical questions as east from west, yet they were to each other as father and son.

The other feature was one which in fact was a characteristic of his whole life. His active brain would not allow him to confine his thoughts to the routine of work, but prompted him to extend his reading and writing to many subjects of historic and theological interest. The result of this was seen in the publication from time to time of papers, poems, and essays, of the comforting little book entitled *The Spiritual Doctrine of Recognition in the World to Come,* and, later, of the careful and original study of the marriage relations under the title *Husband and Wife.* But at this time his reading and his interest in child life drew him into the study of that singular episode of the middle ages, the Children's Crusade. With characteristic industry he read the ancient chronicles in the libraries of Europe and this country. His linguistic talent, his familiarity with the continent of Europe, and his imagination were brought into service. So that from the volumes which had been gathering dust for centuries he sketched a vivid picture. From his pages we catch sight of tens of thousands of children gathering together in France and Germany at the call of the Boy Preachers. We follow that strange army over the Alps and hear from the cliffs the echo of the crusaders' hymns; we pass the bodies of hundreds of children resting, weeping, sick, and dying from cold and hunger. We accompany them to the Mediterranean and watch the ships disappear below the horizon; and then we weep at their betrayal, shipwreck, and bondage to the Saracens whom they had gone forth to conquer.

The story breathes with pity and love for these misguided children, and is a revelation of the author's tender, sympathetic heart.

In 1876 Dr. Gray was elected to the position of Dean of the Episcopal Theological School in Cambridge.

The school was founded upon the basis of justification by
faith and the evangelical principles which Dr. Gray professed.
But many people had read into these noble terms a spirit of
partisanship and exclusiveness which did not belong to them.
Moreover, Cambridge was popularly considered to be the hot-
bed of all forms of rationalism and infidelity. Evangelicalism
in the home of rationalism gave glorious opportunity for the
critics and enemies of the institution. The school, while her-
alded as rich, was at about that time borrowing money to pay
its running expenses and was in danger of closing its gates from
poverty. Dr. Stone, one of the noblest of that noble band of
leaders of the evangelical school of the Church, had just resigned the position of Dean in order to pass his declining years
in a well-earned rest. It was a difficult post; and it called for
a man of courage and devotion to accept it.

On the seventeenth day of May, the new Dean took up his
residence in Cambridge and entered upon his duties.

In his administration it would have been easy for Dean Gray
to have appealed to party spirit for his support and to have let
the school run its life out with the party.

In his relations to the spirit of Cambridge, it might have
seemed natural for a man of his inherited traits and mental
training to have steeled himself against its influence or to have
held himself aloof from its contact. But such was not the man.
He was from New Amsterdam and not from New England,
he was born a Presbyterian and not a Puritan, he was orthodox
to the backbone and not a rationalist, he was provincial and
Cambridge is provincial; but back of all he was a gentleman,
a scholar, and a Christian. Dogmatic in manner, he was in fact
receptive of new truth. Strongly set in argument, he would
feel the truth in the reasoning of the other side, and in time
would unconsciously absorb what he had denied in debate. He
gradually allowed himself to breathe more and more of the
atmosphere with which he was surrounded. No! I hardly do

him justice in this expression. The keynote of his life was, as I said at the beginning, intellectual and spiritual development.

Realizing, perhaps before he came here, certainly soon after his coming, that the line of thought in which he was moving must lead into wider fields, he set to work to discover them.

His duties as professor gave him a special stimulus in reading, thought, and spiritual development. His knowledge of other languages, especially of German, came to his aid and opened up hitherto unknown vistas of religious thought. Sometimes his omnivorous reading seemed to overwhelm his thought. Soon the old system which was hemming in the man showed signs of breaking before the fresh light; and then with the passing of years came new and grander views of God, of the church, and of mankind. His conversation, teaching, and preaching revealed the movement, but his Baldwin Lectures, written in the midst of and in spite of the fatal disease which was sapping his life, give the most mature expression of his thought.

His whole conception of religion became more ethical and spiritual. His study of the person of Christ led him to a deeper realization of the Catholic doctrine of the Trinity as the basis of religious faith; the doctrine of the Incarnation took on wider and deeper relations; the Atonement became less mechanical and more spiritual; the fact of Christ's Resurrection rose to a position of higher and higher significance in his preaching and teaching; the truth of the present, living Christ and of the energizing power of the Holy Spirit in the church received new emphasis.

He was led by his study of evidences and of modern thought and life to a higher and higher appreciation of the historic church, her institutions, and her Catholic creeds. But there was one note which he struck with all the persistency and strength at his command, the Catholicity of the church. He thus speaks in one of his Baldwin Lectures:

If anything is evident, it is that the Church shows that it is Apostolic and Catholic by endorsing no Theology and committing itself to no scientific results. There are many systems or schools of Christian thought within the allowable limits of adherence to the Creed and Prayer Book. There are many theories of particular subjects, such as sacraments, ministry, atonement, eschatology, and others more or less important, many theories even of the very organization of the Church. But the Church identifies itself with none, regards all as only approximate at the best, and authorizes no man to speak for it as to the final definition of anything.

Of course much of this was and is in the air; thousands are drifting into freer light; but it was not in him to drift. If he was not a leader of religious thought in the larger meaning of the term, he was by his reading and thought close onto the heels of the leaders, and through his voice and action the men and students behind him were kept in touch with the advance. He did not move rashly, he loved truth too much to tempt her with foolhardy statements and experiments, and he loved men and their faith too dearly to unsettle them before he had a better truth to give.

The development of his thought made itself felt in his work as a teacher. His was not the single eye of the scholar seeking truth for truth's sake only; he was in too close touch with life for that; he sought it also for man's sake, and he brought it quickly to men's use. This eagerness to teach combined with his active temperament was sometimes a drawback, inasmuch as it did not allow him to wait for the slower working of the student's mind; he kept well in the lead. If he was restless at what he felt to be unreasonable dullness and spoke quickly, the aggrieved student always knew that behind the voice was the tender heart and the large spirit; and whatever his opinion on that point, the student had full confidence in the man. It was this that drew to him the loyalty of every young man that passed through these gates. His reverence for the truths he taught and his respect for the sacredness of his calling restrained his sense of humor in the class room. But what was thus lost by him was gain for the students in the realization of the awfulness of treating sacred themes.

A man with such convictions and with Dean Gray's strength of character could not, with a sympathetic faculty, help having a marked effect upon the growth of the Institution. In his annual report for the year 1885–86, he gives his conception of the spirit of this school:

> This, then, is what the School stands for: candid, advanced, unpartisan, manly preparation for the Ministry of CHRIST in this comprehensive Church. Nothing else will long be tolerated by the present growing spirit of the Church. No other method will be submitted to by these young men who have tasted the mental culture and activity of our own region. None other is feasible in the presence of a great University, where men have learned to think for themselves, to distinguish between divine revelation and human opinion, and to appreciate the rich birthright of freedom that is theirs who belong to our Historical Communion. This method alone, as all signs indicate, is to prevail in the large future now opening before our Church. To this conception of our work we shall try to be true.

If one would gain an insight into what Dean Gray felt to be the cardinal features of the ministry which this school hopes to cultivate, he may find it in his last report:

> Our aim, besides the development of the spirit of consecration and the laying of a sound foundation in the branches pursued, is, according to our ability, to inspire those under our influence with certain deeply imbedded conceptions of the Ministry, as essential to the work to which they are called in this day and land. . . . It must be a ministry that is, above all, devoted to CHRIST, not merely in the usual sense thereof, but in the sense of a clear apprehension of His isolatedness as the Revealer and Redeemer. . . . This requires a clear apprehension of the truth and the nature of those fundamental tenets of Christianity, which are yet but one, the Trinity in Unity, the Incarnation of the Eternal SON, His Atonement, and the justification of men by His merits alone. These truths, if they are to be preached in an age that so much needs them,

are to be studied with the aid of the latest and deepest researches into every quarter whence light can come. . . . The minister, furthermore, must be loyal to the Church whose Orders he receives. . . . The clergy-man must be manly, not only superior to puerilities, but one who can be trusted for his integrity as well as respected for his sagacity. . . . Once more the minister must be thoroughly in sympathy with this land and this people.

He here and in his whole bearing, to quote from one who knows whereof he speaks, "presents an ideal lofty and inspiring, which appeals to all that is honorable and manly in the student, to his conscience and to his reason, which, if carried out, would raise up for the Church a type of ministers commanding respect for their office by the respect freely conceded to their character."

I know of no better testimony to his success as an administrator than the facts that our halls are today filled with a body of students who are, we believe, worthy of his hopes, and that we have a body of alumni, high in character and usefulness, loyal to the school and to the church, men in whom he gloried and whom he loved as a father does his sons. The memory of that last parting at the alumni dinner in June, where a broken voice and silence told more than words, will ever remain as a benediction to the school. That evening was, as he himself described it, his "Pisgah." He had led the school up within sight of great hopes, but it was not given him to enter in.

But we cannot forget that he had other duties than that of Dean.

Filling the chairs of Homiletics and Pastoral Care as well as that of Theology for several years, he was also the pastor of a large congregation in this chapel; and many of them know better than I can tell how his powers matured and his sympathies deepened with years. It was the one regret of his position here that his other duties prevented him from a fuller devotion to his pastoral work, though how he accomplished what he did was a mystery to those who knew him best. He felt strongly that personal contact leads to better understanding and closer sympathy. He therefore made it a duty as well as a pleasure to meet in social or spiritual gatherings the clergymen of his own church and of other Christian bodies. As the Dean of the Eastern Convocation, a member of the Diocesan Board of Missions, a Deputy to the General Convention, and as a member of the Advisory Committee on the Mexican Mission, in which he took a deep interest, and in many other ways he discharged his duty to the church at large. What he was to his brethren in the ministry many of you well know. His last act before sailing to Bermuda, a very sick man, was to collect a fund with which to send a brother clergyman, who seemed to have less chance of life than himself, to a southern climate. He has passed to his reward, but the recipient of his bounty still lives and joins with us here in this service in gratitude to God for the kind and noble heart.

He was one of those who crowded the hours with work, for to work was the joy of his life; to be obliged to cease from work and become a care to others was his great dread. Months ago when he first realized his illness he exclaimed, "Well, if it is God's will that my work shall end here and now, I am ready!" Crowded with engagements, faithful in his duties as citizen, clergyman and Dean, he was more, far more than a man of engagements and duties and work. The fireside of the Deanery was the center of his life's joy and interest. It belonged to him, to his family and, I may almost say, to all men. The college boy, coming from a happy home, found here his second home; and young Harvard graduates throughout the country look to that house with gratitude for their warm reception. The theological student seldom entered that he did not find another before him. The Deanery was the school's hospital, for there the sick student was carried. The western bishop, the missionary, the traveler, all found the same welcome. To neighbors, friends, and strangers as well, the door stood ever open. And even the study door was rarely, I may say never, shut.

It was a home where envy, sordid ambition, and petty rivalries were unknown. His genial heart, his humor, his sense of honor, his sympathy with all that is pure, lovely, and of good report were caught by all who entered.

> Friend of the open hand, the genial eye,
> The lip that faltered never—

Thank God for thy life.

But God's call came and found him ready. The strong frame was weakened, the voice broken, the eyes darkened, and the hand ceased to write, but the man remained. In his weariness he longed for rest. He breathed the words:

> O Paradise, O Paradise,
> 'T is weary waiting here.

And on the fourth day of August, when the light of a Sunday morning was breaking over the peaceful hills of Sharon, the hour of his release came, and (to use his own favorite expression in speaking of the Christian's death), he fell asleep.

He rests from pain and distress, but "glad with the joy of God's countenance," still lives and works. His life reminds us that the joy of labor exists beyond the veil, and his voice, so familiar within these walls, now seems to say:

> GOD hath other fields
> Than those ye know. His sunlight and His rain
> Fall not alone on the remembered earth;
> But here, as there, the duteous harvest yields
> Reward to all; and I am glad again,
> Tilling the land of this my newer birth.